FOODS THAT MADE
Wisconsin
FAMOUS

150 GREAT RECIPES

RICHARD J. BAUMANN

Editor: Stan Stoga
Designer: Kate Orenberg
Cover Photograph: Paskus Photography
Back Cover Photograph: Milwaukee Sentinel, April 30, 1992, Jeffrey Phelps; ©1999 Journal Sentinel Inc., reproduced with permission.

Library of Congress Catalog Card Number: 99-70831
ISBN: 0-915024-70-5
Printed in the United States by McNaughton & Gunn, Inc.

Wisconsin Tales & Trails, Inc.
P. O. Box 5650
Madison, WI 53705
(800) 236-8088
info@wistrails.com

To my dear, sweet wife, whom I love dearly (if only she'd stay out of my kitchen).

To my daughter, Dawn, who lives in Alaska but often requests recipes by e-mail, and to my granddaughter, Alyeska, who is too young to cook but knows a good cookie when she eats it.

To my daughter, Wendy, who lives nearby and often requests that I make a dessert for one of her many dinner parties. And to my grandchildren, Katarina, Anais, Franz, and Michael (Max), two of whom (Anais and Max) have been guests on my TV cooking shows. Their performances were engaging, especially when they suggested that I wasn't doing something correctly (as if they knew, right?).

TOMMY G. THOMPSON

Governor
State of Wisconsin

G R E E T I N G S !

Among the many good things that Wisconsin has to offer, its tasty and healthy food products represent the very best. Wisconsin produces a vast variety of foods, many of which have their origins in the ethnic backgrounds of the first settlers who came here in the mid-1800s and even earlier. Richard J. Baumann's book, The Foods That Made Wisconsin Famous, describes the origins, qualities, and uses of these good Wisconsin foods in a humorous and interesting presentation.

As Governor of the great State of Wisconsin, I am proud of the many wonderful things this state of ours has to offer. Wisconsin cuisine is certainly at the top of that list and should be recognized for its wholesomeness, as well as its taste. The Foods That Made Wisconsin Famous is not just another cookbook – it is a true celebration of good Wisconsin food and how to prepare it. I recommend it to anyone who enjoys the simple pleasures of food, from good cooking to good eating!

TOMMY G. THOMPSON
Governor

TGT/nmb

Room 115 East, State Capitol, P.O. Box 7863, Madison, Wisconsin 53707 ● (608) 266-1212 ● FAX (608) 267-8983

INTRODUCTION

About ten years ago, I took a Cajun cooking class in New Orleans. The program was excellent, but as I was listening and watching the cook give his demonstration, the thought flashed through my mind, "Wisconsin has every bit as much to offer both in good cooking and in food products as does his Louisiana!"

When I returned to Wisconsin I established the Wisconsin School of Cookery. I developed and presented programs that were designed to be snappy, fast-paced, entertaining, and informative and would provide a taste of Wisconsin featuring "the foods that made Wisconsin famous" (just as Schlitz beer became "the beer that made Milwaukee famous").

Now, many programs later (including a television series), all I know and love is contained in this book. Well, okay, maybe not *all*! What I thought I knew about Wisconsin food and cooking, I double-checked and verified. And what I didn't know, I researched until I found it and again double-checked and verified.

Although I wanted to make the book as historically accurate as possible, I did have a few problems along the way. Where I found vastly conflicting dates in my research, I simply phrased them as "around the 1800s" or whatever time period they fell into. Where specific dates appeared consistently in my research, I used those specific dates, confident that they were correct.

My concept of the final book was to provide cooks and readers with an overview of the major categories of Wisconsin's foods—not just the cheese and beer that comes to everyone's mind when Wisconsin food is mentioned. People often ask me, "What else is there besides cheese and beer?" Well, there's a whole lot more, and it's all in this book.

The organization of the book is geographical. The first six chapters discuss the foods of the six major regions of the state, as designated by the Wisconsin Department of Tourism. The food overview of each region provides a "feel" for and familiarization with certain foods and why they are predominant in the area (for example, ethnic composition or soil conditions). Then specific foods are discussed in more detail, and recipes for them follow. Many foods are common throughout the state and are not necessarily exclusive to one spot. These are mentioned in chapter 7.

So whether you're a cook looking for recipes or a reader wanting to know more about Wisconsin foods, this book should satisfy your interests. The book is readable, the facts and information are interesting without being academic, and the recipes are clear, precise, and easy to follow. I have tried to avoid ultra "haute cuisine" or outlandish recipes that take a great deal of preparation time or call for obscure or hard-to-find ingredients.

The recipes I have chosen fall into a category that might be dubbed "honest cooking" — simple, straightforward, and well within any cook's expertise or lack thereof. I hope that experienced cooks will rediscover some cooking basics and find the recipes interesting enough to add to their collection of sophisticated cuisine. I also hope that both the novice cook and the everyday practical family cook will feel inspired and challenged to cook something a bit different but still in keeping with family tastes.

Many of the recipes combine a variety of Wisconsin ingredients, and this blending results in a distinct character that makes Wisconsin cooking as unique as southern cooking, Cajun cooking, or other such well-known cooking styles.

The recipes are tried-and-true; they come from my family, from friends, and from various other sources (a governor or two, a restaurant or two, recipe contest winners, food associations, food growers and processors, and the Wisconsin Department of Agriculture). We can't go wrong on all of those, now, can we?

All the recipes have a common thread: they are Wisconsin's best foods and provide delicious dishes for real people with hearty appetites, discriminating tastes, and unpretentious expectations.

So, if you're a Wisconsinite, re-examine or rediscover what the state's foods have to offer. If you're from another state, come on over—join us and enjoy!

SOUTHERN GATEWAY
CHAPTER ONE

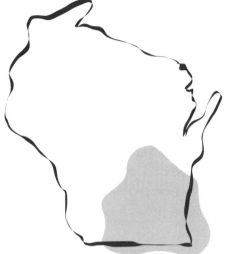

DANE

DODGE

JEFFERSON

KENOSHA

MILWAUKEE

OZAUKEE

RACINE

ROCK

WALWORTH

WASHINGTON

WAUKESHA

The southeast portion of Wisconsin was indeed a gateway to the settling of the rest of the state. Just choose your country or culture—its people were there. Many stayed on permanently in the area, while others remained only until they could afford to move and settle elsewhere. They all brought with them a rich heritage of cooking, and their combined recipes for a vast array of foods have made Wisconsin famous.

Large numbers of Germans, Swiss, British, Cornish, and Irish came in the mid-1800s. Germans predominated and settled mainly on farms in Milwaukee, Ozaukee, and Washington Counties. They felt that a farm was an important family possession and a permanent, forever-place to live. Some of those who preferred not to farm—but stayed permanently in Milwaukee—went on to brew beer, make sausage, and operate bakeries that sold schnecken, stollen, tortes, kuchen, Bismarcks, and a great variety of breads, including semmel and hard rolls.

The late 1800s and early 1900s saw a deluge of immigrants from Norway, Sweden, and Denmark as well as from Italy and Poland; in lesser numbers many other nationalities—Hungarians, Czechs, Serbs, Croats, Russians, and even a free-Black community—also settled during this period. By the time Wisconsin became a state on May 29, 1848, it was the most ethnically diverse state in the union, and until 1910 at least one-third of the population was foreign born.

Many of the Danish people settled in the Racine area, while the Norwegians located primarily around Stoughton in Dane County. Of all the Scandinavians in Wisconsin, Norwegians made up the largest group and their specialty was tobacco culture. In this connection, they are credited with originating the first coffee break. Housewives worked in the tobacco sheds and periodically went home to check not only on their children but also on any food they might have had simmering on the stove for the evening meal. While at home, they poured a cup of coffee, so this time away from work became known as the coffee break. Today's worker doesn't have to go home to check the kids or tend to a meal, and the coffee break is a time to socialize and relax. Whether employers appreciate it as much as employees do, it has become an integral part of everyday life.

By the 1870s cooking schools began to emerge in the larger cities. Classes provided information and instruction in store-bought food versus home-grown food, on basic food preparation, and on menus and recipes designed to improve the diets of the new immigrants and the poor. In 1896 the publication of Fannie Farmer's *Boston Cooking-School Cook Book* revolutionized cooking by providing standardized measures and precise instructions for all recipes. Its influence and the conviction that "doing good works" and providing clothing for the needy were not enough moved Elizabeth Black Kander and others in Milwaukee to establish a curriculum of classes and a cooking school within an organization known as The Settlement. To save the time and effort spent copying the day's lessons on a blackboard, Lizzie (as she was known) decided to get the lessons and recipes printed, and to pay the printing costs she and her committee solicited advertisements. In April 1901, they published a 174-page book containing more than 525 traditional American and Continental recipes culled from the committee members and the students themselves. (It also included twenty-four lessons on such topics as Setting the Table, Rules for a Household, How to Bone a Fish, and General Rules of Mixtures Using Baking Powder.) *The Settlement Cookbook: The Way to a Man's Heart* was born and, with continual revisions and updating, it has remained as much a classic as Fannie Farmer's cookbook and an important contribution to American cooking.

With the growing concentration of people in the area as well as the influx of new immigrants, a social activity of previous centuries re-emerged. Aztecs had held annual "great fairs" in Mexico City, and even the Romans had introduced fairs to Northern Europe.

Initially, they were an all-male activity for showing off prize livestock and farm crops, but they soon also became festive social events. The first recorded fair in the American colonies took place in 1644 in New Haven, Connecticut. The first Wisconsin State Fair was held in October 1851 in Janesville, and shortly thereafter it was moved to Milwaukee, a much more populous area. In fact, Abraham Lincoln gave a speech at the Wisconsin State Fair in Milwaukee in 1859. It remains an enormously popular event, with its countless booths featuring many different authentic ethnic cuisines. The Wisconsin Bakers Association's cream puff booth, however, is probably the most popular.

These are only the highlights of the contributions of immigrants of all nations to today's Wisconsin menu. Their influences are even reflected in so-called junk food. Who hasn't dipped into a bag of Tostitos, Doritos, or nachos (Mexican origin), or grabbed a handful of pretzels (German)? Rock County, Wisconsin, is known as the Junk Food Capital of the World for its concentration of potato chip, corn chip, caramel corn, and related food manufacturers.

We experience today the best of all ethnic cooking, whether in its purest ethnic origin or as a co-mingling of several countries. We end up with a world-class cuisine that not only is unique but can modestly be called "A Glorious Celebration of Wisconsin Food."

BEER

Picture this: Many thousands of years ago a caveman was out on an extended hunt. It rained, his cave roof leaked, water soaked into the stored grain, and the grain fermented. Caveman returns and tastes the soupy mess—he likes it! Happy hunting has existed ever since. Today, however, beer making has become a bit more sophisticated.

Beer and bread have the same basic ingredients, so it was no surprise that in medieval Europe, brewing beer and making bread went hand-in-hand. Since women were the bakers, guess who were the brewers?

Originally, everyone drank beer (no ID needed) for practical reasons—the alcohol killed some of the bacteria present in the drinking water. By the seventeenth century, when brewing became commercially successful, men took over the operation, leaving the women to continue baking their bread.

In the 1840s when the first big wave of Germans came to the United States they brought a yeast different from the kind the English used for their ales and stouts. Since beer drinking was woven into the very fabric of German culture and since the Milwaukee area was heavily German (by 1900, 72 percent of Milwaukee's population was German), it was not surprising that enterprising Germans who stayed in the area established breweries.

His name is nearly forgotten and no brewery is named after him, but the very first beer maker in Milwaukee was Richard Griffith Owens, who established the Milwaukee Brewery in June 1840. After that, the brewing frenzy began. Four years after Owens set up his brewery, Phillip Best switched his factory from vinegar to beer production. His son-in-law Frederick Pabst joined him 22 years later. Frederick Miller started his brewery in 1855. Joseph Schlitz was a bookkeeper when he took over the brewery of August Krug, another forgotten name in beer history. When the Great Chicago fire wiped out the city's water supply in 1871, Schlitz Brewing Company sent hundreds of barrels of beer to thirsty Chicagoans. This generous act inspired the slogan "Schlitz, the beer that made Milwaukee famous." Unfortunately Joseph Schlitz was lost at sea in 1875. To keep the brewery

operating, his widow brought in her four nephews, the Uihlein brothers.

It's interesting to note that during Prohibition, Pabst began to produce a nonalcoholic beer, and Schlitz started the Eline Chocolate Company. (To add a bit of family trivia: As a young man, my father-in-law worked for the Eline company for a number of years until he was fired for putting too many nuts into a batch of candy.) Since Eline Chocolates didn't put Hershey out of business as planned, the Uihleins ventured into banking. When Prohibition was repealed, they resumed brewing.

Germans loved their beer and singing, hospitality and good times, and even the sound of the German word for it (*Gemuetlichkeit*) sums up the entire concept very nicely. Capitalizing on this, most breweries set up biergartens as social centers where families could relax, socialize—and drink beer, of course. The breweries also bought up corner properties to establish taverns where their beer was sold exclusively. The corner tavern is still a mainstay of many neighborhoods.

We tend to think of beer almost solely as a drink, but it is also an excellent ingredient in cooking. One doesn't even need a recipe to use beer. Just substitute beer for part of the water. Beer works especially well in anything that requires a long cooking time. It also has some thickening properties that come from the interaction of the heat and the yeast content of the beer. The hops in beer provide the taste and aroma. Since the hops flavor becomes stronger as the beer evaporates, American beers are generally better for cooking than foreign beers, which usually use stronger hops. Beer is not alcoholic when used in cooking because at 80 degrees F., the alcohol evaporates and leaves only the other ingredients to flavor the food. And for the diet conscious, a 12-ounce bottle or can of beer has only 140 calories; a soft drink has up to 170 calories, and just 2 ounces of gin in your favorite Martini has 142 calories. So choose your beverage carefully.

Beer continues to quench many a thirst, whether served at a backyard picnic or at an exclusive country club. It's equally appropriate in the kitchen for cooking purposes.

BEER CHEESE SOUP

INGREDIENTS

3/4 cup butter (1 and 1/2 sticks)

1/2 cup celery, finely chopped (approx 1 stalk)

1/2 cup carrot, finely grated (approx 1 medium size carrot)

1/2 onion, finely chopped

1/2 cup all-purpose flour

4 and 1/2 cups chicken broth (use canned broth if you don't have any chicken stock OR use a
  chicken soup base; bouillon cubes are not recommended because they are too salty)

2 tablespoons Parmesan cheese, shredded

6 oz sharp cheddar cheese, grated (mild is okay, but sharp will give the soup a better taste)

1 bottle or can of beer (12 oz size); a lite beer is not recommended since it lacks body

1/2 teaspoon dry mustard

PROCEDURE

- Melt butter in soup kettle and sauté vegetables until limp, but not brown.
- Stir in flour all at once; continue stirring over low heat until flour expands—
  you'll see it happen!
- Gradually add the chicken broth, stirring constantly until thickened and then
  simmer for 5 to 10 minutes.
- Blend in the Parmesan and cheddar cheeses and beer and stir until all the cheeses
  have melted.
- Add the dry mustard and salt/pepper to taste.
- Simmer at least 10 minutes before serving.

NOTES

Preparation and cooking time take about 25 minutes. This is a very rich soup; if too thick, some
warm milk may be added. Garnish with a sprinkle of paprika, chopped parsley, or croutons.
Recipe may be cut in half, since this one will provide 10 to 12 servings.

EXTRA-LIGHT BEER BISCUITS

INGREDIENTS

2 cups all-purpose flour, sifted

3 teaspoons baking powder

1/2 teaspoon salt

3 tablespoons sugar

4 tablespoons cold shortening

1 can or bottle (12 oz size) of flat/stale beer at room temperature

> (Flat/stale beer is decarbonated beer which can be achieved by leaving an opened can or bottle stand overnight OR, to immediately remove the carbonated gases, pour the beer through a coffee filter.)

PROCEDURE

- Combine dry ingredients.
- Cut-in the shortening with pastry blender.
- Pour in beer and mix until well blended.
- Drop dough portions directly into muffin tins OR roll out dough, knead, cut, and place on baking sheet.
- Bake at 375 degrees until golden brown.

BEER BATTER

INGREDIENTS

1 and 1/3 cups all-purpose flour, sifted

1 teaspoon salt

1 tablespoon melted butter

2 eggs, separated; save whites

3/4 cup flat/stale beer (see Extra-Light Beer Biscuits recipe on preceding page)

PROCEDURE

- Combine flour, salt, butter, egg yolks, and beer and beat until smooth.
- Cover and set aside in cool place.
- Beat egg whites until they are stiff and fold into batter.
- Dip seafood, chicken, onion rings, or vegetables into batter and fry.

NOTES

Don't overbeat the batter, and let it rest for a short period before using. Make sure that whatever you are coating is absolutely dry so that the batter will cling. Beer is an excellent ingredient in any batter since it produces a lighter batter.

QUICK BEER BATTER

INGREDIENTS

1 can or bottle (12 ounces) beer
1 cup all-purpose flour, sifted
1 tablespoon salt
1 tablespoon paprika

PROCEDURE

- Pour beer in mixing bowl; combine flour, salt, and paprika and sift into the beer.
- Whisk the batter until light and frothy.

NOTES

Will keep a week or more in the refrigerator.

HAM BAKED WITH BEER

INGREDIENTS

1 precooked ham
Whole cloves
1/2 cup packed brown sugar
1 tablespoon dry mustard
2 tablespoons vinegar
2 cups beer

PROCEDURE

- Score ham and insert cloves.
- In small bowl make a paste of sugar, mustard, and vinegar.
- Spread paste over ham.
- Pour beer in bottom of roasting pan.
- Bake at 350 degrees for 1 and 1/2 hours, basting frequently.

CHICKEN IN BEER

INGREDIENTS

1 chicken cut in pieces
1/2 cup all-purpose flour
1 teaspoon salt
1/4 teaspoon pepper
3 or 4 tablespoons butter
1 onion, sliced thin
1 can or bottle (12 ounces) beer at room temperature
1/2 cup heavy cream
Fresh parsley, chopped

PROCEDURE

- Combine flour, salt, and pepper and dip chicken pieces into mixture, coating evenly.
- Melt butter in large skillet over medium-high heat.
- Add onions and chicken and fry, turning often to cook evenly until the pieces are nice and brown (about 15 minutes).
- Add beer, lower heat, and cover.
- Simmer for about 40 minutes, periodically turning the chicken pieces.
- Mix cream and chopped parsley directly into skillet with chicken, raising heat back to medium high and cook for another couple of minutes.
- Remove chicken pieces to serving platter.
- Whisk the sauce in the skillet to thoroughly combine and pour over chicken.
- Serve immediately.

SHRIMP IN BEER

INGREDIENTS

2/3 pound shrimp (Determine the total weight by the size of each shrimp and the number of
    people to be served. Also, see the notes to determine the amount of beer and water
    to be used.)

2 cans or bottles (12-ounce size) of flat/stale beer
    (for flat/stale beer, see Extra-Light Beer Biscuits, page 5)

8 ounces water

12 peppercorns

2 bay leaves

1/2 teaspoon celery seed

PROCEDURE

- Shell and devein shrimp.
- Combine all ingredients and bring to a boil.
- Drop shrimp into boiling beer mixture.
- Partially cover and simmer for about 7 minutes—just until shrimp are pink.
- Drain, cool, and serve.

NOTES

More or less beer and water may be used, depending on the amount of shrimp to be cooked—
the proportions are 3 parts beer to 1 part water.

BEER COOKIES

INGREDIENTS

1 cup beer
1 cup raisins
1 stick butter, softened
1 cup packed brown sugar
2 large eggs
2 cups all-purpose flour
1/2 teaspoon allspice
1 teaspoon baking soda
1/2 teaspoon salt
1/2 teaspoon vanilla
1/4 teaspoon almond extract
1 cup chopped walnuts
1/2 cup grated coconut

PROCEDURE

- Cook raisins in beer for a few minutes to plump them.
- Drain and reserve 1/2 cup of the liquid.
- Cream butter and sugar and beat until fluffy.
- Add 1 egg at a time and beat well.
- Sift together flour, allspice, baking soda, salt; mix in batter and gradually add reserved beer, a little at a time.
- Add vanilla and almond extracts, raisins, walnuts, and coconut; mix thoroughly.
- Drop spoonfuls about 2 inches apart on greased cookie sheet.
- Bake at 350 degrees for about 12 to 15 minutes until light brown.

BEER CHEESE DIP

INGREDIENTS

8 ounces softened cream cheese

1/2 to 3/4 cup beer

8 ounces sharp cheddar cheese, cubed

1 clove garlic

12 small sweet gherkin pickles, chopped

    (these are the small dark green cucumbers, pickled in vinegar)

1 teaspoon poppy seeds

PROCEDURE

- Combine cream cheese and 1/2 cup beer in blender for a few seconds.
- Add cheddar cheese cubes and garlic and blend until smooth.
- Add remainder of beer if a thinner consistency is desired.
- Add gherkin pickles and poppy seeds and blend a few seconds.

NOTES

Preparation time is about 10 minutes. Makes about 3 cups.

BEER CHEESE SPREAD

INGREDIENTS

2 cups sharp cheddar cheese, shredded

2 cups Swiss cheese, shredded

1 teaspoon Worcestershire sauce

1/2 teaspoon dry mustard

1 small clove garlic, minced

1/2 to 2/3 cup beer

PROCEDURE

- In medium-size bowl, combine all ingredients except beer until well blended.
- With beater, add enough beer to bring mixture to a spreading consistency.

NOTES

Excellent served on rye bread or assorted crackers. Makes about 2 cups.

BEER BLOODY MARY

INGREDIENTS

1 and 1/2 ounces vodka

1 teaspoon lemon juice

3 ounces flat/stale beer (for flat/stale beer see Extra-Light Beer Biscuits, on page 5)

V-8 brand juice

Tabasco or Worcestershire sauce, as desired

Celery salt

Celery stalk or dill pickle

PROCEDURE

- Combine vodka, lemon juice, beer, and V-8 in appropriate size glass.
- Add Tabasco or Worcestershire sauce to taste.
- Stir and fill glass with ice cubes.
- Sprinkle celery salt on top.
- Garnish with celery stalk or dill pickle.

NOTES

Makes 1 drink.

SAUERKRAUT

Most people associate sauerkraut with Germany, but it really originated in China, of all places! The builders of the Great Wall fed the workers rice and cabbage. In winter the cabbage was preserved in rice wine, where it fermented and became sauerkraut. (I don't know what the Chinese called it!) Tartar warriors under the leadership of Genghis Khan invaded Europe and carried cabbage with them, fermented in a salt brine. It soon became a staple and a favorite food in the conquered areas now known as Germany. An interesting historical footnote: During World War I, the German word sauerkraut was replaced with the words *liberty cabbage* as a patriotic gesture.

Sauerkraut is low in calories (42 calories per cup), rich in fiber, and a good source of vitamin C, but it is high in sodium because of the salt needed to ferment it. The salt content—as well as tartness—can be reduced by first rinsing the kraut in cold water.

While Wisconsin ranks only sixth in production of small cabbages for the fresh market (harvested in July), it ranks first in growing big cabbages for sauerkraut (harvested in mid-September). Wisconsin sauerkraut accounts for 40 percent of all U.S. production.

My grandmother used to make sauerkraut in a stone crock, which she kept in the basement. She placed a round, tight-fitting board on top of the shredded cabbage and brine and a fairly heavy stone on top of the board to keep out air. Anyone making sauerkraut today could substitute a plastic bag filled with water for the board and stone. My mother used to send me down to the basement with a saucepan to fill with the evening vegetable. I always used to grab a "sniggle" of kraut between my thumb and two fingers and shove it in my mouth to eat on the long climb back upstairs—I loved it cold! I think our sauerkraut crock was kept in the basement to keep it cool and out of the way, but an old book that gave sauerkraut-making instructions specifically said, "Don't store in the bedroom." The book explained that fermenting kraut makes an incredible amount of noise as bubbles echo against the side of the crock and it bubbles irregularly, which is not "conducive to sleep."

Sauerkraut shouldn't be thought of only as a vegetable. It is extremely versatile and adaptable to any type of cooking and can be used in many recipes as a unique and flavorful ingredient. For full flavor, just heat the kraut. For a more interesting and mellow flavor, add a little brown sugar, chopped apple, and onion and simmer slowly until heated thoroughly.

CREAMY REUBEN SOUP

INGREDIENTS

1/2 cup onion, chopped

1/4 cup celery, chopped

3 tablespoons butter

1/4 cup unsifted all-purpose flour

3 cups water

4 teaspoons beef-flavored soup base (or 4 beef bouillon cubes)

1/2 pound corned beef, shredded

1 cup sauerkraut, drained and rinsed

3 cups half and half cream

12 ounces Swiss cheese, shredded

6 to 8 slices rye or pumpernickel bread, toasted and cut into quarters

PROCEDURE

- In large saucepan cook onion and celery in butter until tender.
- Stir in flour until smooth.
- Gradually stir in water and beef soup base (or bouillon cubes) and bring to a boil.
- Reduce heat and simmer uncovered 5 minutes.
- Add corned beef, sauerkraut, half and half cream, and 1 cup shredded Swiss cheese.
- Cook 30 minutes until slightly thickened, stirring frequently.
- Ladle into oven-proof bowls.
- Top each bowl with toasted bread and the remaining shredded Swiss cheese.
- Place bowls under broiler until the cheese melts and serve immediately.

NOTES

Preparation time is about 20 minutes, plus 45 minutes cooking time. Serves 8.

SAUERKRAUT SALAD

INGREDIENTS

1 can (27 ounces) sauerkraut, drained and rinsed

1/2 cup celery, chopped

1/2 cup green bell pepper, chopped

1/2 cup onion, chopped

1/2 cup carrot, shredded

1/2 cup sugar

1/2 cup red wine or cider vinegar (a red wine vinegar is best)

1/2 teaspoon salt

1/3 cup vegetable oil

PROCEDURE

- Combine first 5 ingredients in large bowl.
- In small bowl, whisk sugar, vinegar, salt, and vegetable oil.
- Pour whisked mixture over sauerkraut mixture and mix well.
- Cover and chill at least overnight.
- Drain and toss before serving.

NOTES

This will keep in the refrigerator for 2 weeks.

BREWED SAUERKRAUT

INGREDIENTS

3 strips bacon, diced

1 cup onion, chopped

2 pounds sauerkraut, drained and rinsed

2 tablespoons brown sugar, packed

1/2 teaspoon caraway seeds

1 can or bottle beer (12 ounces)

Pepper to taste

1 cup carrot, coarsely shredded

PROCEDURE

- Fry diced bacon in large skillet until crisp.
- Remove bacon, drain, and set aside.
- In same skillet with bacon grease, add onions and sauté.
- Stir in sauerkraut, sugar, caraway, beer, and pepper.
- Bring to a boil, then reduce heat, cover pan, and simmer for one hour.
- Add carrots and simmer uncovered until carrots are tender (about 20 minutes).
- Put in serving bowl, garnish top with crisp diced bacon bits.

NOTES

Serves 6.

SAUERKRAUT POTATO CASSEROLE

INGREDIENTS

6 large potatoes, boiled with skins on

3 or 4 tablespoons milk

5 tablespoons butter

Salt and pepper

1 small onion, sliced

1 pound sauerkraut, drained and rinsed

2 tablespoons Swiss cheese, grated

PROCEDURE

- Remove skins from cooked potatoes while still warm and mash, adding milk, 2 tablespoons butter, salt, and pepper and beat until fluffy (basic mashed potatoes).
- Place one half of the mashed potatoes in the bottom of a buttered 1 and 1/2-quart casserole.
- Sauté the sliced onion in 1 tablespoon butter until soft.
- Add sauerkraut, cover, and simmer 10 minutes.
- Spoon onion/sauerkraut mixture over top of potatoes in the casserole.
- Add remaining potatoes on top of that.
- Spread grated Swiss cheese on top and dot with the remaining 2 tablespoons of butter.
- Bake uncovered at 350 degrees for about 35 minutes, uncovering the last 10 minutes.

NOTES

Makes 6 to 8 servings

SAUERKRAUT IN WINE

INGREDIENTS

2 pounds sauerkraut, drained and rinsed
2 tablespoons butter
1 cup water
1/3 cup dry white wine

PROCEDURE

- Melt butter in heavy covered pan and add sauerkraut.
- Cover and cook over lowest heat for 1/2 hour.
- Add water and wine and continue cooking (covered) 1/2 to 1 hour longer.

NOTES

Leftover champagne is an excellent substitute for the wine. Serves 6 to 8.

SAUERKRAUT PORK CHOPS

INGREDIENTS

1/4 pound bacon (hickory smoked recommended)

6 loin pork chops about 1 inch thick

2 pounds sauerkraut, drained and rinsed

1 jar (15 ounces) chunky applesauce (regular is okay, but chunky is preferred)

1 tablespoon brown sugar

1 teaspoon dry mustard

1/4 cup dry white wine (or champagne)

Dash pepper

1/4 teaspoon paprika

PROCEDURE

- Dice bacon and sauté until crisp; drain on absorbent paper.
- Sauté pork chops separately until golden brown on both sides.
- Mix diced bacon, sauerkraut, applesauce, brown sugar, dry mustard, wine, and pepper.
- Place 1/2 of the sauerkraut mixture in bottom of shallow 9 x 12-inch casserole.
- Place pork chops on top of mixture and cover chops with remaining sauerkraut mixture.
- Sprinkle with paprika.
- Cover and bake at 350 degrees for 1 hour.

NOTES

This is an excellent dish; a pork chop and the sauerkraut mixture can be served onto the dinner plate directly from the casserole dish. A green vegetable is an excellent accompaniment. Makes 6 servings.

SAUERKRAUT CRANBERRY MEATBALLS

INGREDIENTS

Meatballs

2 pounds ground beef

2 eggs

1 envelope onion soup mix

1/2 cup water

1 cup finely crushed saltines

Sauce

1 can (14 to 16 ounces) sauerkraut, drained, rinsed, and finely chopped

1 can (8 ounces) cranberry sauce (whole or strained)

3/4 cup chili sauce or ketchup (chili sauce is preferred)

2 cups water

1/3 cup brown sugar

PROCEDURE

- Mix together ground beef, eggs, onion soup mix, 1/2 cup water, and crushed saltines.
- Form into meatballs (golf ball size if this is to be used as a main dish; smaller if as an hors d'oeuvre).
- Brown meatballs in slightly oiled or greased skillet.
- When browned, remove from pan and set aside.
- Mix together the sauerkraut, cranberry sauce, chili sauce or ketchup, 2 cups water, and brown sugar.
- Pour half of the sauerkraut mixture in a 9 x 13 (or similar size) pan.
- Arrange meatballs on the sauce and pour remaining sauce over the top.
- Cover pan with foil and bake at 350 degrees for 1 hour.
- Remove foil and if too juicy, bake another 15 to 30 minutes, but watch so that it doesn't dry out.
- Serve over mashed potatoes, noodles, or rice, if desired.
- If serving as an hors d'oeuvre, do not bake the additional 15-30 minutes (you want the meatballs to remain moist in the juice).

CHOCOLATE SAUERKRAUT CAKE

INGREDIENTS

1 and 1/2 cups sugar

2/3 cup butter

3 eggs

1 teaspoon vanilla

2 and 1/4 cups all-purpose flour

1 teaspoon baking soda

1 teaspoon baking powder

1/2 cup unsweetened cocoa

1 cup cold water

2/3 cup sauerkraut, drained, rinsed, and chopped fine

PROCEDURE

- Cream sugar and butter until blended and smooth.
- Add eggs and vanilla and beat until fluffy.
- Mix dry ingredients in separate bowl.
- Add dry ingredients to creamed mixture with the water and beat until completely blended.
- Stir chopped sauerkraut into batter.
- Pour into 2 greased and floured 9-inch round layer pans OR greased and floured 9 x 13 cake pan (I often use a bundt pan).
- Bake at 350 for 25 to 30 minutes for layer pans and 35 to 40 minutes for larger pan or bundt pan. (If center of cake in bundt pan is still too moist but top seems to be done, I cover the bundt pan lightly with a piece of foil so the center will get done without the top getting too crusty.)
- The layers or 9 x 13 cake can be frosted with the classic frosting:
    - 3 ounces cream cheese, softened
    - 6 tablespoons butter, softened but not melted
    - 1 teaspoon vanilla
    - 2 cups powdered sugar
    - 1 tablespoon milk
- Blend cream cheese and butter; add all other ingredients, and beat until smooth; add milk if necessary to make frosting spread more easily.
- Shaved chocolate (using a vegetable peeler and baking chocolate squares) on top makes for a nice finish.
- For a bundt cake, powdered sugar (sprinkled through a wire sieve) is all that is needed.

SAUERKRAUT DIP/SAUCE

INGREDIENTS

1 cup sauerkraut, drained and rinsed

1 cup plain yogurt (do not use flavored yogurt) OR 1 cup mayonnaise

PROCEDURE

- Puree sauerkraut.
- Add yogurt or mayonnaise and blend until smooth.

NOTES

This can be used as a dip or as a sauce over baked potatoes, meats, or fish. For a variation, you may add chili sauce, taco sauce or Tabasco sauce, or your choice of herbs. This unusual recipe came from a University of Wisconsin Extension bulletin, and the food science professor who concocted it called it *Kole*. *Kole* is the German word for cabbage.

KRINGLE

In Denmark the word *kringle* referred to cookies and tea cakes made with butter. There was such a concentration of Danish people in the early days of Racine that the area became known as Kringleville. The kringle they made, however, consisted of very thin layers of dough and butter glazed with brown sugar and cinnamon, a filling of pecan, apples, dates, prunes, or cheese, and sugar icing. An authentic kringle is difficult to make. Once the dough is mixed and kneaded, each layer must be buttered and folded three dozen times. Then it must rest in the refrigerator for three days before it is shaped, filled, and glazed. It can be served warm or at room temperature. An additional slather of butter makes something already rich and scrumptious even more so.

The oldest family kringle bakeries in Racine are Bendtsen's (four generations) and the O & H Danish Bakery (more than 50 years old). For folks who would like to have a kringle hot out of the oven, a frozen bake-and-serve version was introduced in April 1998 by His Day Foods of Racine. It's called Oliver's Kringle.

Racine is said to be the only place in the United States that makes kringle, and I believe it! I've scoured dozens of cookbooks, food dictionaries, and the like and found no mention of kringle, much less a recipe. This is surprising because the few authentic kringle bakeries in Racine do a huge mail order business, shipping to all parts of the U.S. as well as stocking kringles in grocery stores (at least in Wisconsin). The following "make-at-home" kringle recipes are probably not as good as an authentic Danish bakery kringle, but they are very good homemade substitutes.

QUICK & EASY DANISH KRINGLE

INGREDIENTS

Dough

1 and 1/2 packages (1/4-ounce size) dry yeast

2 cups all-purpose flour

1/2 cup shortening

1 tablespoon sugar

1/2 teaspoon salt

1 egg

1/2 cup milk

Filling

1/2 cup (1 stick) butter

3/4 cup sugar (use equal parts white and brown sugar)

1 teaspoon cinnamon

Pecans, ground or chopped

Additional options for filling: raisins, chopped apple, prunes, almonds; canned pie filling can also be used, but some of the liquid will have to be drained.

PROCEDURE

Dough

- Mix yeast, flour, shortening, sugar, and salt as for pie crust, only finer.
- Mix the egg in the milk.
- Blend egg/milk mixture all at once with dry ingredients.
- Cover and refrigerate overnight.
- When ready to bake, divide dough into 3 parts and roll out as thin as possible.

Filling

- Mix softened butter and all other ingredients.
- Spread filling down the center, fold over ends and sides to cover filling.
- Put seam-side down on cookie sheet lightly sprayed or coated with oil.
- Leave kringle long or shape into a crescent.
- Bake at 350 degrees for 1/2 hour or until light brown.
- Sprinkle with powdered sugar while still warm.
- Chopped nuts can also be sprinkled on the top, if desired.

NOTES

Makes 3 kringles but dough can be divided into 2 for larger ones or 4 for smaller ones.

These freeze nicely and need only to be thawed or warmed.

NO-YEAST KRINGLE

INGREDIENTS

2 cups all-purpose flour

1 cup sour cream OR 8 ounces cream cheese, softened

1 cup (2 sticks) butter

PROCEDURE

• Same as for Quick and Easy Danish Kringle on preceding page.

NOTES

Instead of a powdered sugar topping, a glaze can be made by combining 1 tablespoon melted butter, 1 tablespoon milk, and 1 teaspoon vanilla.

CREAM PUFFS

The ingredients of this all-American delight are simple: eggs, milk, flour, water, and salt. Elsewhere in the world, Italians fill their version with ricotta cheese (cannoli), the French fill it with vanilla cream and a chocolate topping (eclair); and the English fill their puff with currants and spice. In Wisconsin they're filled with none other than genuine dairy fresh whipped cream and dusted with powdered sugar. The pastry shell is good by itself, but it's that whipped cream filling that makes it a cream puff. I might add that the only way to eat it is with hands—certainly not with a knife and fork. And yes, the whipped cream oozes out all over your face and fingers, but what an uninhibited way to enjoy something so good.

The Wisconsin Bakers Association set up a model bakery to showcase dairy products at the Wisconsin State Fair in 1924. Never mind the competition from cakes and cookies; cream puffs were a big hit and are definitely here to stay. Records show that by the end of the 1997 fair, a total of 220,000 cream puffs had been sold. That amounts to more than 30 per minute. One out of every four persons attending the State Fair eats a cream puff. If all their cream puffs were laid end to end, they would stretch 14 miles. Lots of smeary faces, but lots of happy smiles.

A restaurant in Minocqua, in Northern Wisconsin, serves its cream puff with the top set askew and calls it a knee cap. It makes another version from fried doughnut batter. Both are filled with whipped cream and sprinkled with powdered sugar. The knobby appearance of both does resemble a knee cap.

WISCONSIN STATE FAIR CREAM PUFFS

INGREDIENTS

1 cup water
1/4 teaspoon salt
4 tablespoons (1/2 stick) butter
1 cup all-purpose flour, sifted
4 eggs
1 egg yolk, lightly beaten
2 tablespoons milk
2 cups whipping cream (add vanilla extract and sugar to taste)
Powdered sugar

PROCEDURE

- Butter and flour 1 very large or 2 small baking sheets or line with parchment paper.
- Pour water and salt into very large saucepan.
- Cut butter into small pieces and add to water; cook over medium-low heat so butter melts before water boils; then bring water just to boiling point.
- Remove saucepan from heat and add flour all at once, stirring vigorously with a wooden spoon until dough forms into a ball and bottom of pan is filmed with flour.
- Let dough rest 5 minutes.
- Add whole eggs, beating in one egg at a time. Dough should be stiff, but smooth.
- Immediately drop 1/4 cupfuls of dough 3 inches apart on baking sheet (or for a neater appearance, use pastry bag with 3/4-inch plain tip and pipe dough onto baking sheet).
- Combine egg yolk and milk in a small bowl and brush each puff with mixture, being careful not to let liquid drip onto baking sheet.
- Bake at 375 degrees for 35 minutes, until puffed, golden brown, and firm.
- Cool puffs on wire racks, pricking each with a cake tester or toothpick to allow steam to escape, OR leave them in a turned-off oven with the door propped open for about an hour, until firm.
- Cut tops off thoroughly cooled puffs and fill with whipped cream with a large spoon or pastry bag.
- Replace puff tops and sprinkle with powdered sugar.

NOTES

Baked puffs should have hollow, moist interiors and crisp outer shells that are lightly browned. If the puffs are filled before they are cool and firm, they will be soggy and may collapse. Makes 12 cream puffs. This is the official recipe of the Wisconsin Bakers Association from the 1924 Wisconsin State Fair.

MINIATURE CRABMEAT-FILLED CREAM PUFFS

INGREDIENTS

1 cup water
1/2 cup (1 stick) butter
1/4 teaspoon salt
1 cup all-purpose flour
4 large eggs

Crabmeat Filling

1 can (7 and 1/2 ounces) crabmeat, drained (Cooked lobster, shrimp, or tuna can be used instead of crabmeat.)
1 package (8 ounces) cream cheese, softened
1 tablespoon green onion, finely chopped
2 tablespoons almonds, toasted and finely chopped
2 teaspoons Worcestershire sauce

PROCEDURE

- Bring water, salt, and butter to a boil in medium-size saucepan and then remove from heat.
- Stir in flour all at once and beat well until mixture leaves the sides of the pan.
- Cool for 1 minute, add eggs one at a time, beating after each addition—mixture should be smooth and glossy.
- Drop tablespoon-size amounts on greased baking sheet.
- Bake at 450 degrees for 15 minutes and then reduce heat to 350 and continue to bake an additional 25 to 30 minutes until puffs are golden brown with dry, rigid sides.
- Remove from baking sheet and place on wire rack to cool, making a slit in the side of each puff with a knife.

Filling

- Place all ingredients in blender and blend until smooth.
- Extra onion, garlic powder, or onion powder may be added to the filling mixture, if desired.
- Grated pepper cheese can be put in the bottom of the puffs before the filling is added, if desired.
- When ready to serve, fill puffs and bake at 350 degrees for 15 minutes; serve hot.

NOTES

This is an excellent hors d'oeuvre. Makes about 25 to 30 miniature puffs.

CREAM PUFF SWANS

INGREDIENTS

1 cup milk

1 stick butter, cut into small pieces

1 teaspoon sugar

Dash salt

1 cup all-purpose flour

4 large eggs

PROCEDURE

- In medium saucepan, over moderately high heat, combine milk, butter, sugar, and salt until butter is melted and water has just reached the boiling point.
- Remove from heat and pour in flour.
- Stir vigorously until dough forms a ball and leaves sides of pan.
- Return to heat and stir 1 to 2 minutes to dry out the dough.
- Remove from heat and make a well in the center of the dough.
- Add eggs 1 at a time, beating after each addition.
- After the last egg, beat a minute longer until dough is smooth and shiny.
- Lightly grease baking sheet and drop heaping tablespoons, making 10 two-and-one-half-inch mounds, leaving enough room to allow for expansion. (Reserve some dough for Swan Necks.)
- Bake at 400 degrees for 25 to 35 minutes until golden brown.
- Cool in oven 1 hour with door ajar.

Swan Necks
- Pipe dough in the shape of an S on lightly greased baking sheet and bake 10 minutes until underside is golden.

NOTES

To assemble swans: Cut off top 1/3 of the rounded part of the puff and cut that in half. (These will be the wings of the swan.) Fill cream puffs with whipped cream. Insert swan neck on one end of the puff and place a wing on each side. These cream puff swans make an especially nice dessert for a baby shower if the whipped cream is tinted with blue and pink food coloring (assuming one wants a traditional boy/girl motif). For a spring or summer dessert, tint the cream with yellow; for Thanksgiving, an orange tint; and, of course, for Christmas, a darker green or red tint. I often make a batch of swan necks separately and freeze them for future use; when I need them, just the cream puffs have to be made.

CHOCOLATE

Wisconsin doesn't grow cocoa beans, but it certainly contributes to the world's joy of chocolate. On May 9, 1894, a German-born Milwaukeean, Otto Schoenleber, started producing chocolate after his furniture business failed. (This was coincidentally the same year that Hershey's began.) Otto named his company Ambrosia, since chocolate was known as the "food of the gods." He began making penny candies but after World War I concentrated on producing large quantities of cocoa powder to be sold commercially to other candy and cookie manufacturers. Ambrosia still exists, and its outlet store is a favorite place for home cooks and bakers to buy a wide variety of chocolate products.

The town of Burlington in Kenosha County is the home of a Nestlé chocolate-producing facility and holds an annual chocolate fest in May. The first one in 1987 featured the world's largest candy bar weighing 1,631 pounds, as well as a 1,291-pound crunch bar.

At the second fest, they outdid themselves with a 2,756-pound chocolate colossus—that's two million times the size of the ordinary half-gram morsel used in chocolate chip cookies. Unique chocolate creations have been a feature each year—in 1992 it was a 2,000-pound cow, and in 1998 it was an eight-foot "tree of knowledge" that depicted the history of chocolate. This annual event is a nonalcoholic affair and everyone gets a free chocolate bar. And imagine tromping over the chocolate fest grounds, whiffing the wonderful aroma from the cocoa beans spread underfoot.

In 1988 Hershey Foods challenged Burlington's use of "Chocolate City USA." The confrontation drew national attention and was referred to as the Chocolate Wars. Eventually Burlington won the right to use the title but not on candy packages. But the folks in Hershey, Pennsylvania, can't walk down Nestle Crunch Drive to a chocolate tasting tent—so ha-ha on them!

LOOSEY-MOUSSEY CHOCOLATE CAKE

INGREDIENTS

7 ounces semisweet chocolate

1/4 pound (1 stick) unsalted butter

7 eggs, separated

1 cup sugar (divided 3/4 and 1/4)

1 teaspoon vanilla

1/8 teaspoon cream of tartar

PROCEDURE

- In a small pan, melt chocolate and butter over low heat.
- In a large bowl, beat egg yolks and 3/4 cup sugar until light and fluffy (about 5 minutes).
- Gradually beat in warm chocolate mixture and vanilla.
- In another large bowl, beat egg whites with cream of tartar until soft peaks form.
- Add remaining 1/4 cup sugar 1 tablespoon at a time.
- Continue beating until stiff.
- Fold egg whites carefully into the chocolate mixture.
- Pour 3/4 of the batter into ungreased 9 x 3-inch springform pan.
- Cover remaining batter and refrigerate.
- Bake cake at 325 degrees for 35 minutes, remove, cool on wire rack (cake will drop so don't be alarmed).
- When cake is cool, remove the loose-mousse from the refrigerator and stir to soften.
- Spread loose-mousse on top of cake and refrigerate until firm.
- If desired, top may be covered with whipped cream when served, with grated chocolate for garnish.

NOTES

Place foil or a cookie sheet under the springform pan to catch any leakage in the oven.

CHOCOLATE CHIP MARSHMALLOW TORTE

INGREDIENTS

Crust

1 and 1/2 cups graham cracker crumbs

1/2 cup powdered sugar

1/2 stick butter

Filling

1 cup milk

30 marshmallows, cut up

1 cup whipping cream, stiffly beaten

3 or 4 squares semisweet or unsweetened chocolate, coarsely chopped or grated

PROCEDURE

Crust

- Melt butter.
- Combine with graham cracker crumbs and powdered sugar.
- Cover bottom of 7 x 11 pan and chill, OR bake at 350 degrees for 5 to 6 minutes to obtain a more crisp texture.

Filling

- Heat milk, but do not boil, in medium- to large-size saucepan.
- Add cut-up marshmallows and, over very low heat, stir until they are all dissolved.
- Cool mixture.
- Fold in the stiffly beaten cream and chocolate and pour into crust.
- Chill.
- If desired, top with additional graham cracker crumbs, whipped cream, or a cherry topping.

FUDGE TRUFFLE CHEESECAKE

INGREDIENTS

Crust

1 and 1/2 cups vanilla wafer crumbs (about 35 wafer cookies)

1/2 cup powdered sugar

1/3 cup unsweetened cocoa

1/3 cup butter, melted

Filling

3 packages cream cheese (8-ounce size), softened

1 can sweetened condensed milk (14 ounces)

2 cups (12 ounces) semisweet chocolate chips, melted

4 eggs

2 teaspoons vanilla

PROCEDURE

Crust

- In medium bowl combine wafer crumbs, sugar, cocoa, and butter.
- Press into bottom of 9-inch springform pan.

Filling

- In large mixing bowl, beat cream cheese until light and fluffy.
- Gradually add sweetened condensed milk and beat until smooth.
- Add remaining ingredients and mix well.
- Put into springform pan .
- Bake at 300 degrees for about 1 hour and 5 minutes or until center is set.
- Cool on wire rack.
- Chill and garnish as desired.

NOTES

I lightly butter the sides of the springform pan and swirl around some additional crushed vanilla wafers. I also lightly butter the bottom of the springform pan before I put in the crust mixture to facilitate removal of servings. Place foil under the springform pan to catch any leakage in the oven. This is a very, very rich dessert and is indeed just like a chocolate truffle. A very small dollop of whipped cream on top of each piece is the only garnish needed and would be strictly for appearance.

MILK CHOCOLATE TERRINE

INGREDIENTS

1 pound milk chocolate (use only milk chocolate)
8 ounces whipping cream
1/2 stick butter
1 egg yolk

PROCEDURE

- In double boiler, melt chocolate.
- In separate pan, bring cream and butter to a boil.
- Add cream and butter to the chocolate.
- Beat egg yolk lightly and combine with mixture.
- Line a loaf pan with plastic wrap and pour mixture into pan.
- Refrigerate overnight.
- To remove from pan, turn upside down, remove plastic wrap, and slice.

NOTES

This is a very rich dessert and remains soft, making it difficult to cut. I find it helps to hold the knife under hot water before cutting each slice. This recipe was given to my wife by the chef of the executive dining room of the Inter-American Development Bank in Washington, D.C. Karo syrup put out a similar recipe called Chocolate Truffle Loaf with Raspberry Sauce. While it was basically the same, theirs included powdered sugar and corn syrup, which gave the dessert a bit more body but reduced the pure richness of the bank's recipe The raspberry sauce is a very nice addition: Simply puree a package (10 ounces) of thawed raspberries, strain, and add about 1/3 cup light corn syrup to make the sauce less runny.

CHOCOLATE CREAM CHEESE PIE

INGREDIENTS

Crust

1 cup graham cracker crumbs (reserve 2 tablespoons for garnish)

5 tablespoons butter, melted

1/4 cup brown sugar

1/8 teaspoon nutmeg

Filling

6 ounces chocolate chips

1 package (8 ounces) cream cheese, softened

3/4 cup brown sugar (divided into 1/2 and 1/4 cups)

1/8 teaspoon salt

2 eggs, separated

1 cup whipping cream

1 teaspoon vanilla

PROCEDURE

Crust

• Combine all crust ingredients, pat into bottom of 9-inch pie pan, and chill.

Filling

• Melt chocolate chips and let cool 10 minutes.

• Blend cream cheese with 1/2 cup brown sugar and salt.

• Beat in egg yolks, one at a time.

• Stir in cooled chocolate.

• In separate bowl, beat egg whites until stiff.

• Beat 1/4 cup brown sugar into the egg whites gradually.

• Beat 1 cup whipping cream and add to egg white mixture with vanilla.

• Combine egg white mixture with chocolate mixture.

• Pour into graham cracker crust, sprinkle top with reserved crumbs.

• Chill overnight.

WISCONSIN STATE FAIR GIANT
CHOCOLATE CHIP COOKIES

INGREDIENTS

1/2 pound (2 sticks) butter

3/4 cup plus 2 tablespoons vegetable shortening

1 cup sugar

1 cup packed brown sugar

1/2 tablespoon salt

2 teaspoons vanilla

2 large eggs

2 tablespoons warm water

2 and 1/2 cups flour

2 and 1/2 cups cake flour (to make your own cake flour see notes below)

1 and 1/2 teaspoons baking powder

2 and 1/2 teaspoons baking soda

2 cups miniature milk-chocolate chips, refrigerated

PROCEDURE

- In large bowl, cream butter, shortening, and sugars.
- Add salt, vanilla, and eggs and cream well.
- Add water and mix about 15 seconds, scraping sides of bowl.
- In separate bowl, combine the two flours.
- Sift baking power and baking soda into flour mixture.
- Mix into creamed butter mixture, just until incorporated.
- Stir in chocolate chips.
- Dust hands lightly with flour.
- Divide dough into 16 equal rounds.
- Press flat on a lightly greased or sprayed cookie sheet.
- Cookies should measure about 5 inches in diameter (in the baking process, they will spread to about 6 inches).
- Bake at 350 degrees for 8 to 10 minutes or until cookies are light brown.

NOTES

Makes 16 cookies. This is the official recipe of the Wisconsin Bakers Association from the 1924 Wisconsin State Fair. Cake flour recipes:

Recipe #1: For 1 cup cake flour, combine 3/4 cup sifted bleached, all-purpose flour with 2 tablespoons cornstarch.

Recipe #2: For 1 cup cake flour, measure out 1 cup all-purpose flour and remove 2 tablespoons.

CHOCOLATE BUTTER CRUNCH CANDY

INGREDIENTS

1 cup sugar
1/2 teaspoon salt
1/4 cup water
1/4 pound (1 stick) butter
12 ounces semisweet chocolate
1 cup walnuts, finely chopped

PROCEDURE

- Butter a cookie sheet.
- Combine sugar, salt, water, and butter in a saucepan.
- Bring mixture to a boil over low heat, stirring constantly, until sugar dissolves.
- Cook mixture to 285 degrees on a candy thermometer or the soft crack stage (a little syrup dropped in cold water will form a pliable ribbon).
- Pour boiled mixture onto sheet and cool thoroughly.
- Melt chocolate in double boiler.
- Spread 1/2 of the melted chocolate over cooled mixture.
- Sprinkle with 1/2 of the nuts.
- When chocolate is firm, turn candy over (good luck!).
- Spread turned-over side with remaining chocolate and sprinkle with remaining nuts.
- When hardened, break into pieces.

NOTES

Makes about 1 and 1/2 pounds. When turning the candy over, it is not terribly important to keep it perfectly in one piece, since eventually the candy is broken into pieces.

CHOCOLATE TRUFFLES

INGREDIENTS

1 cup heavy cream

2 tablespoons sugar

1/2 stick butter, cut into pieces

1 pound bittersweet or semisweet chocolate, cut into pieces

1 tablespoon rum or brandy

PROCEDURE

- In heavy saucepan, heat the cream, sugar, and butter until butter is melted and sugar is dissolved (do not boil).
- Remove from heat and add chocolate, stirring until smooth.
- Add rum or brandy and blend.
- Cover and cool slightly (about 10 minutes).
- Set in pan of ice and stir until mixture is smooth and firm.
- Roll teaspoons of mixture (called ganache) into balls and then roll in cocoa, nuts, chocolate sprinkles, or coconut, or dip in chocolate.

NOTES

These are every bit as delicious as the expensive truffles one would buy. They are relatively easy to make.

ADULTS ONLY CHOCOLATE SAUCE

INGREDIENTS

1/2 pound sweet chocolate

1/2 cup brewed coffee

1 tablespoon Cognac

1 teaspoon vanilla

3 tablespoons heavy cream

PROCEDURE

- Break chocolate into small pieces and combine with coffee in saucepan.
- Cook over low heat and stir until melted and smooth.
- Add Cognac, vanilla, and cream; blend.
- If not used immediately, cool, and when ready to use, reheat in double boiler.

DUCK

Wisconsin ranks second in U.S. duckling production, with 45 percent of the annual total of over 21 million ducks. A large duck farm is located in the Franksville area in Racine County. Wisconsin has the highest per capita consumption of ducks, followed by Texas and Florida. As a food, duck dates back to 3000 B.C. when Egyptians considered wild duck a delicacy. The Romans also considered duck a luxury, but ate only the breast and brains. It was the Crusaders who so popularized eating wild ducks that they began to be domesticated in Europe in the 1400s. The duck industry in America began in 1873 when Captain James Palmer brought some Peking ducks to Long Island. The Long Island duckling (a white Peking duck) is the result of selective breeding from nine strains of Peking duck.

Thanks to genetic engineering, farm-raised ducks are no longer "fatty," and more than 60 percent of restaurants serve duck on a regular basis. If you feel that you must get rid of absolutely all fat, simply score the skin of the duck, being careful not to pierce into the meat itself. Whatever fat is there will render off very nicely. Also, when roasting the duck, place it on the rack breast side up so any fat drains away from the meat. Whatever fat exists is in the duck's skin and not in the meat itself. If cooked properly, the skin will be crisp, and even that fat will be eliminated or at least substantially reduced.

Duck has a very succulent flavor, which distinguishes it from other fowl. It's been stated that duck goes "beak to beak" with chicken and turkey when it comes to nutritional content. For example, duck has the same protein as turkey, but the breast meat has twice the iron.

Duck should be baked at 350 degrees for 30 minutes to the pound. If you use a glaze, coat the duck during the last 15 to 20 minutes of roasting. When serving a sauce with duck, it is best to serve it on the side, to allow each person to add sauce to individual taste.

DUCK WITH SAUERKRAUT

INGREDIENTS

1 duck, 4 to 5 pounds
Salt/pepper
1/2 lemon
1 small, whole onion, peeled
2 pounds sauerkraut
2 apples, peeled and chopped
1/2 cup white wine
1/2 cup seedless red grapes
2 tablespoons flour
1 and 1/2 cups water

PROCEDURE

- Sprinkle duck with salt and pepper.
- Rub skin with cut side of lemon.
- Put peeled whole onion in duck cavity.
- Place duck on rack in roasting pan.
- Roast at 350 degrees for 1 to 1 and 1/2 hours (or until meat thermometer in leg registers 170 degrees).
- While duck is roasting, combine sauerkraut, apples, and wine and simmer covered for about 1/2 hour.
- When duck is more than half done, remove from rack and pour off pan drippings into bowl; when the drippings have cooled to room temperature, chill in freezing compartment so the fat will rise to the top and can be easily removed.
- Arrange the sauerkraut mixture in a casserole, place the duck on top of it (or cut the duck into quarters at this point).
- Place grapes over the top of the sauerkraut and around the edges of the duck.
- Place casserole in oven and bake 1/2 hour longer.
- When pan drippings have been cooled and fat removed, add 2 tablespoons flour and blend.
- Add 1 and 1/2 cups water and salt to taste.
- Simmer to make a gravy.
- After the casserole has baked the last 1/2 hour, remove duck to platter and add half the gravy mixture to the sauerkraut; reserve the other half of the gravy for serving.

NOTES

This recipe comes from a hunting lodge near Nuremberg, Germany. Mashed potatoes are an excellent accompaniment.

DUCK ENCHILADAS

INGREDIENTS

1 duck, 4 to 5 pounds

1/2 onion, finely chopped

2 tablespoons oil

1/2 cup chicken stock (a chicken soup base is fine)

1 can (8 ounces) refried beans

1 teaspoon Tabasco sauce

1 cup Monterey Jack cheese, grated

1/2 cup sour cream

2 cups lettuce, julienned

10 corn or flour tortillas

Corn/Bean Salsa

1 cup each: corn, black beans, chopped tomatoes

1 dash Tabasco sauce

PROCEDURE

- Chop uncooked duck into chunks.
- Stir-fry duck chunks with onions in oil until done.
- Add chicken stock and simmer.
- In separate pan, combine refried beans and Tabasco and heat thoroughly.
- Bake tortillas at 400 degrees for 2 minutes and remove.
- Fill tortillas with refried beans and duck.
- Fold tortillas in half, cover with cheese, and return to oven until cheese is melted.

Corn/Bean Salsa

- Heat corn and drain.
- In separate pan, heat black beans with Tabasco, then mix with corn and add tomatoes.
- Serve tortillas on bed of lettuce with sour cream and accompany with the Corn/Bean Salsa.

CROCK POT DUCK WITH GRAND MARNIER ORANGE SAUCE

INGREDIENTS

1 duck, quartered

Salt/pepper

1 large onion, quartered

2 stalks celery, julienned large

3 carrots, julienned large

6 ounces fresh mushrooms, halved

1 tomato, quartered

2 potatoes, medium size, quartered

1 can (10 ounces) beef broth, or make up beef soup base in same amount

Grand Marnier Orange Sauce

1/3 cup brown sugar

1/3 cup white sugar

1 tablespoon cornstarch

1/4 teaspoon salt

1 cup orange juice

1 to 2 (maybe more?) tablespoons of Grand Marnier liqueur

PROCEDURE

- Salt/pepper all sides of duck quarters.
- Place in crock pot.
- Add vegetables and broth.
- Cover and cook on medium heat for 8 hours.

Grand Marnier Orange Sauce

- In medium-size saucepan, combine the two sugars, cornstarch, and salt.
- Slowly stir in orange juice until smooth.
- Heat over low heat and simmer until transparent and thickened (about 3 minutes).
- Add Grand Marnier liqueur.
- Place 1 quarter duck portion on each plate, divide up the vegetables, and ladle Grand Marnier Orange Sauce over duck.

NOTES

Serves 4.

HIDDEN VALLEYS
CHAPTER TWO

CRAWFORD

GRANT

GREEN

IOWA

LA CROSSE

LAFAYETTE

MONROE

RICHLAND

VERNON

Swiss immigrants had been trudging around the Midwest for years, looking for just that right wooded, hilly area that would remind them of their majestic mountain homeland. They finally found that spot in Green County and established the town of New Glarus in 1845. And, oh my, what all did they bring with them: Lace making, woodcarving, watch making, and the best of all—Swiss cheese.

The Swiss wanted a special cheese that would be different from the more than 100 varieties they produced (Raclette, Appenzeller, natural Gruyere, to name a few of the better known ones), so they created one with a distinctive look—it had holes in it. The special culture or bacteria they used created the bubbles and helped produce the hazelnut flavor. They called the cheese Emmentaler, after the Emme Valley in Switzerland, where it originated centuries ago. Today, it is simply called Swiss cheese, and it is the most imitated cheese in the world. Unfortunately, no one thought to protect the name Emmentaler or Swiss, so those names now refer to types of cheese, rather than the place of origin.

Another nationality whose members wanted to settle in an area reminiscent of home were the Norwegians. While Norwegians are in every county of Wisconsin, the greatest concentration is at Mount Horeb (Grant County). Three miles west is Little Norway, a re-created Norwegian village of a century ago. The sandy creek bottoms in the valleys provided the ideal soil composition to grow potatoes for making their beloved lefse (potato pancakes) and, of course, a Norwegian feast always consists of pickled beets, creamed cabbage, and lutefisk.

In Norway, lutefisk was made from cod caught in the North Sea, split into "sides," dried in the mountains, and then softened for a number of days in lye water and finally soaked for a long time in brine. Supposedly, only a Norwegian cook knows exactly when to remove the fish from the brine for the best flavor. While some Wisconsin Norwegian communities might even have lutefisk festivals, it really isn't something most people would make at home, and the taste for it is "acquired."

Figuring prominently in both culture and food were the Cornish. Lead mines in Cornwall, England, had become exhausted in the early 1800s and news of a fabulous lead strike at Mineral Point, Wisconsin, in 1828 brought thousands of Cornish to the area. Mining was big for about twenty years until the discovery of gold in California in 1848 caused over half of the miners to leave Wisconsin for California.

The Cornish contribution to Wisconsin foods is the pasty (if you remember that it rhymes with nasty, you won't confuse it with a burlesque queen's accessory!). Basically, a pasty consists of vegetables baked in a pie crust. It often had a triangle shape to fit into a miner's pocket, making it easy to pull out for lunch or supper while deep in the mine. Sometimes the miner's wife dropped the pasty forty or fifty feet down the mine shaft, so the crust had to be sturdy enough to withstand the impact. Maybe now, a delicate, flaky crust might be more appropriate, but heated arguments still persist over the correct ingredients and whether to cover the pasty with gravy (assuming it's being eaten on a plate and not dropped down a mine shaft). I have the feeling that the original pasties were filled with whatever vegetables were available from the Cornish garden.

The heart of Wisconsin's apple-growing region is in the valleys of the Gay Mills area. Wisconsin produces about 50 million pounds of apples and ranks No. 17 in the nation. At one time, every farm had its own orchard but this is generally no longer the case. The first commercial orchards were planted between 1830 and 1850 and are now found in over half of Wisconsin's seventy-two counties. They total eight thousand acres and yield close to 1.5 million bushels annually (seems to me we should rank higher than seventeenth!). Well over a hundred varieties are grown and harvested between August and October. While the most popular are Jonathan, Golden Delicious, and McIntosh, I like the romantic names of some of the

early varieties, now long forgotten: Maiden Blush, Pumpkin Sweet, Willow Twig, and the intriguing Northern Spy.

A more recent wave of immigration resulted in the settlements of the Amish. Eastern Vernon County is home to Wisconsin's largest Amish settlement. Their farms are picture perfect and their black lacquered buggies are drawn by well-groomed horses. They are easily identified by their dress, the white caps for the women and the black hats for the men. Amish pies, preserves, and other foods are excellent.

The Hidden Valleys region offers a delightful visual experience of beautiful hills and valleys and an equally delightful culinary experience—from the apples on their trees to the perennial specialties of the Swiss, Cornish, Norwegians, and Amish who have settled there.

APPLES

The Wisconsin Apple Growers Association gleefully shouts, "Apples fill you up, not out!" Even the old adage "An apple a day keeps the doctor away" reinforces the fact that apples are indeed healthful. They are an excellent source of pectin (a type of fiber), which limits the cholesterol the body absorbs and may be an important link in preventing heart disease. They are also an excellent dieter's food since a medium apple is sweet and yet has only eighty calories.

The word *apple* comes from the Old English *aeppel*. While apples have been known by most civilizations for thousands of years, there were no native American apples when the first settlers arrived. The pilgrims brought the first apple seeds in 1620. The French brought the apple to Canada, and the cultivation of apples stretched from there down into the thirteen colonies. Long Island, New York, had the first commercial orchard in 1730, and about a hundred years later commercial orchards were planted in Wisconsin. Because of Wisconsin's short growing season and severe winter, a special kind of apple tree had to be developed. Today, after years of trials and failures, the most popular Wisconsin apples are the McIntosh, Cortland, and Red Delicious.

Even though U.S. consumers eat about 65 apples (or 22 pounds) per person annually, there is still an overabundance of them. About one half of the total crop is processed into other apple products—applesauce, pie filling, jams, jellies, and juices.

For a totally enjoyable experience in autumn, drive the country roads resplendent in fall colors, happen onto a farmer's roadside stand, taste an apple, and take home a brimming bag, secure in knowing that these farm-fresh, plucked-right-off-the-tree apples are outstandingly delicious!

APPLE & BUTTERNUT SQUASH
SOUP

INGREDIENTS

1 butternut squash (approximately 1 pound)

3 tart green apples (Granny Smith), peeled, cored, coarsely chopped

1 medium onion, coarsely chopped

1/4 teaspoon rosemary

1/4 teaspoon marjoram

3 cans condensed chicken broth

2 cans water

2 slices white bread

Salt/pepper to taste

1/4 cup heavy cream

1 tablespoon fresh parsley, chopped (for garnish)

PROCEDURE

- Cut squash in half, peel, seed, and cut into chunks.
- In large, heavy saucepan combine squash, apples, onion, herbs, broth, water, bread, salt, and pepper.
- Bring to boil and simmer uncovered for 45 minutes.
- Purée mixture in blender 2 cups at a time until smooth.
- Return pureed soup to saucepan, bring to a boil, and reduce heat until ready to serve.
- Just before serving, blend in cream.
- Garnish each bowl with the chopped parsley.

NOTES

This recipe is from a good friend who is one of the best cooks I know.

HEAVENLY APPLE SALAD

INGREDIENTS

Cake

1 cup nuts

1 cup sugar

1/2 pound dates, chopped

1 teaspoon baking powder

2 tablespoons (heaping) flour

1 egg

Fruit

4 oranges

4 apples

1 and 1/2 cups sugar

8 bananas

Whipped cream

PROCEDURE

Cake

- Mix together all ingredients.
- Bake in a greased 9 x 13 cake pan at 350 degrees until golden brown (about 15-20 minutes).
- Let cool and then crumble in large bowl.

Fruit

- Chop apples and oranges.
- Combine with sugar and let sit overnight.
- Pour mixture over crumbled cake.
- Slice bananas on top.
- Top with whipped cream.
- Refrigerate until ready to serve.

NOTES

This recipe won first place in the 1986 apple recipe contest sponsored by the Wisconsin Apple and Horticultural Council and the Wisconsin Department of Agriculture.

OAT BRAN APPLESAUCE
MUFFINS

INGREDIENTS

2 and 1/2 cups oat bran cereal, uncooked

1/4 cup brown sugar

1/4 cup walnuts

1/4 cup raisins

1 tablespoon baking powder

3/4 cup skim milk

4 egg whites

1/3 cup honey

3 tablespoons vegetable oil

1/2 cup applesauce, unsweetened

1/8 teaspoon almond flavoring

1/2 teaspoon cinnamon

PROCEDURE

- Grease bottoms of 2 medium-sized muffin pans, OR line with paper baking cups.
- Combine all dry ingredients.
- Add milk, egg whites, honey, oil, and applesauce.
- Add all remaining ingredients.
- Fill cups 3/4 full.
- Bake at 350 degrees for 15 to 17 minutes until golden brown.

NOTES

This recipe won second place in the 1989 apple recipe contest sponsored by the Wisconsin Apple Growers Association and the Wisconsin Department of Agriculture. Makes 12 muffins.

APPLE BREAD

INGREDIENTS

2 whole eggs, plus 2 egg whites, slightly beaten

2 cups sugar

1 cup vegetable oil

1 tablespoon vanilla

3 cups flour

1 teaspoon baking soda

1 teaspoon salt

4 cups apples (McIntosh suggested), finely chopped

1 cup pecans, chopped

Topping

2 tablespoons sugar

1/2 teaspoon cinnamon

PROCEDURE

- Grease and flour two 9 x 5 loaf pans.
- Mix eggs, sugar, oil, and vanilla.
- Sift flour, soda, and salt.
- Add to egg mixture and mix well.
- Stir in apples and nuts.
- Divide batter evenly between the two loaf pans.
- Sprinkle each with the topping.
- Bake at 350 degrees for 1 hour and 10 minutes or until cake tester comes out clean.
- Remove from oven and let bread cool in pans for 10 minutes.
- Remove from pans and cool on wire racks.
- Wrap tightly and store at room temperature.

NOTES

If bread isn't done after 1 hour and 10 minutes, place a piece of foil lightly over the top until bread is done. This allows the center to bake without making the edges of the bread crusty. This bread freezes well. This recipe won third place in the 1997 apple recipe contest sponsored by the Wisconsin Apple Growers Association.

APPLE BUTTER

INGREDIENTS

4 pounds of tart apples, cut into pieces (do not peel or core)

2 cups apple cider

1 and 1/2 cups honey

1/8 teaspoon salt

2 teaspoons cinnamon

1 teaspoon cloves

1/2 teaspoon allspice

1 lemon, grated rind and juice

PROCEDURE

- Cook apples in the apple cider until soft.
- Put through a sieve.
- Measure pulp and add remaining ingredients to each 6 cups of pulp.
- Cook total amount uncovered until thick and smooth, stirring carefully from bottom to prevent sticking.
- When cool, store in refrigerator.

NOTES

Can be frozen. This recipe won second prize in the 1991 apple recipe contest sponsored by the Wisconsin Apple Growers Association and the Wisconsin Department of Agriculture.

GERMAN-STYLE
APPLES & CABBAGE

INGREDIENTS

4 cups red or green cabbage, shredded

3 cups tart apples, peeled and sliced

1/2 cup red or white onion, sliced

1/2 cup water

1/4 cup cider vinegar

1/2 teaspoon salt

1 tablespoon sugar

Coarsely ground pepper, to taste

PROCEDURE

- In heavy saucepan, combine shredded cabbage, sliced apples, and onion.
- Add water to cover.
- Cook over medium heat until vegetables become slightly tender (about 8 minutes).
- Add remaining ingredients and continue to cook another 7 to 8 minutes.
- Add more water if necessary to keep vegetables from sticking.

NOTES

This is an excellent accompaniment for pork, beef, or game. Serves 6.

APPLE CRUNCH

INGREDIENTS

5 to 6 apples, peeled and sliced

1 cup flour

1 cup sugar

1 teaspoon baking powder

3/4 teaspoon salt

1 egg, beaten

1/3 cup (5 to 6 tablespoons) butter, melted

Cinnamon

PROCEDURE

- Place sliced apples in a greased 6 x 10 baking dish.
- Mix together flour, sugar, baking powder, salt, and egg.
- Sprinkle mixture over apples.
- Pour melted butter over the top.
- Sprinkle cinnamon over the top of that.
- Bake at 350 degrees for 35 to 40 minutes.

NOTES

This recipe is from my kindergarten teacher, Miss Brown, who helped us prepare a Christmas cookbook for our mothers, which I must admit took place more than sixty years ago. It probably won't win any awards, but it's simple (and good) and gives me a happy nostalgic feeling and I'm happy to share it with you.

NUTTY APPLE CHEESE CRISP

INGREDIENTS

6 cups apples, peeled and thinly sliced

1/4 cup brown sugar

1 teaspoon cinnamon

1 cup apple juice

2 tablespoons lemon juice

1 box cake mix, your choice of white or yellow

3/4 cup peanuts, chopped

1 cup cheddar cheese, grated

1/2 cup butter, melted

PROCEDURE

- Arrange apple slices in ungreased 9 x 12 glass baking dish.
- Mix sugar and cinnamon and sprinkle over apples.
- Combine apple and lemon juices and pour over apples.
- Set mixture aside.
- Combine cake mix, peanuts, cheese, and butter.
- Stir until well blended (it should be crumbly).
- Sprinkle over apples.
- Bake at 325 to 350 degrees for 45 to 50 minutes until lightly browned and bubbly.

NOTES

Can be served warm or cool. A whipped cream topping sprinkled lightly with cinnamon makes a nice appearance. This recipe won first place in the 1994 apple recipe contest sponsored by the Wisconsin Apple Growers Association and the Wisconsin Department of Agriculture.

AMARETTO APPLES WITH MERINGUE

INGREDIENTS

4 medium cooking apples, peeled and sliced

1/3 cup Amaretto liqueur

1/4 cup water

1/2 teaspoon lemon peel, finely shredded

1 tablespoon lemon juice

1 three-inch piece of stick cinnamon

3 egg whites

3 tablespoons sugar

PROCEDURE

- In medium saucepan, combine Amaretto, water, lemon juice, and cinnamon stick.
- Bring to boil; add apples and return to boil.
- Reduce heat, cover, and simmer for 8 to 10 minutes or until apples are just tender, stirring occasionally.
- Remove from heat; let apples stand in cooking liquid for 15 minutes.
- Remove cinnamon stick.
- In smaller bowl, beat egg whites until soft peaks form.
- Gradually add 1 tablespoon of the apple cooking liquid, lemon peel, and sugar.
- Beat on high speed until stiff peaks form.
- Divide the apple slices and the cooking liquid among six 6-ounce custard cups.
- Top each cup with egg white mixture.
- Bake at 325 degrees about 10 minutes or until meringue is light brown.

NOTES

This recipe won first place in the 1990 apple recipe contest sponsored by the Wisconsin Apple Growers Association and the Wisconsin Department of Agriculture.

DUMPLINGS

Dumplings are a universal food. While the name may be different, virtually every country has some sort of food based on a dough mixture filled with fruit or meat. It might be dropped into water and boiled or into oil or fat and fried. There are as many variations as countries. To name a few: Italy, gnocchi; France, quenelles; Austria, specknodle; Korea, mandoo; Israel, matzo.

Refinements of additions of meats, cheeses, or vegetables can even catapult the very simple, easy-to-make dumpling into a main course.

But of all the countries and all the sophisticated variations, none is more dear to my heart than the Swiss *spaetzle*, which means "little sparrow." I love all the Swiss cheeses, but I love my spaetzle even more — could it be because my ancestry is 100 percent Swiss? My grandparents came from Altdorf, Switzerland, the little village made famous by the William Tell episode.

When my Aunt Vic cooked spaetzle, she made a heavier dough by adding more flour; then she rolled it into ropes as round as a quarter and cut off portions and dropped them directly into a kettle of boiling water. She called them buttons, or the German word *knopfli*, because they looked like buttons. I prefer a lighter "button" so I add less flour to my dough mixture, and since it is more on the soft side, I find that taking out small amounts of dough with a teaspoon and dropping them into the boiling water works perfectly. I also like the chunky shapes produced that way—they look like large baroque pearls. If I want a uniform dumpling, I use my spaetzle machine, but then the dough has to be even looser, otherwise it won't go through the holes when the hopper is moved back and forth over the boiling water.

Spaetzle can be made days in advance. I lightly butter a 9 x 12 cake pan, and as the spaetzle come out of the hot water I drop them in the pan. With each successive batch I move them around a bit with a spatula so all of the spaetzle are butter coated. If they are not going to be used immediately, I cover and store them in the refrigerator until needed. They can be reheated in butter on top of the stove or in the oven, and then served plain or with poppy seeds. I prefer simply to brown the spaetzle in some butter, occasionally stirring them, so that all the spaetzle get a nice golden brown coating. If reheated just plain, then some browned bread crumbs on the top make a nice presentation, as well as providing additional taste.

SWISS
SPAETZLE

INGREDIENTS

1 egg
1/2 teaspoon salt
1/4 cup water OR milk (which will make them lighter)
3/4 cup flour
1/4 teaspoon baking powder

PROCEDURE

- Mix all ingredients.
- Drop by spoonfuls into salted boiling water.
- Cook until they float to the surface.

NOTES

Most spaetzle recipes have the same ingredients, but this recipe is direct from my Aunt Vic (now more than 90 years old), who learned it from her Swiss immigrant mother. This makes a small batch and can be easily scaled up for larger amounts. Spaetzle can be made days in advance and kept refrigerated. I like them fried in butter and topped with browned bread crumbs or sometimes poppy seeds.

POTATO DUMPLINGS

INGREDIENTS

2 cups riced potatoes

2 tablespoons butter, melted

Pepper to taste (white pepper won't show specks; black pepper will)

2 eggs, beaten

Milk, about 2 tablespoons

Flour, approximately 1 cup

PROCEDURE

- Combine cooled potatoes, butter, pepper, and eggs.
- Add milk.
- Add flour and combine with potato mixture. More flour may have to be added. The mixture should be firm enough so balls can be made without falling apart when placed in the boiling water. Dumplings may be formed by hand and in any size. I find an ice cream scoop works well. After I scoop out the potatoes, I gently press and roll the potatoes in my palms into nice round balls.
- Drop into salted boiling water and cook gently 6 to 8 minutes.
- Serve immediately.

NOTES

This is my mother-in-law's recipe. The real trick is to get the right amount of flour mixture into the balls—too little and the dumplings will break apart, too much and they'll taste too floury. My wife loves these with a beef roast and rich, brown gravy slathered not only over the meat but also over the dumplings. If I have any dumplings left over, I refrigerate them. The next day I slice them and fry the slices carefully in butter.

PASTIES

Good old-fashioned meat and potatoes are the essential ingredients of a pasty filling. The meat is generally ground beef but some use pork or flank steak. Diced potatoes, rather than sliced or cubed, probably work best, considering the confines of the wrap-around crust. There seem to be as many versions for pasty fillings as there are chili or meat loaf recipes, so do as the early Cornish settlers did—if you like carrots, add 'em; if you like onion, add it, and if you're into rutabagas (beggies) as many Cornish were, add them too. As for the shape of the crust, take your pick: pocket-size triangles, wrap-around diaper-style, or maybe even a crescent shape with crimped edges. Some folks (to the horror of pasty purists) pour ketchup over the pasty; others prefer ladling on some gravy—after all, it is meat and potatoes, right? Do what you like, but if you visit a restaurant in Mineral Point (the heart of Cornish country in Iowa County) that features authentic Cornish pasties, you might be well advised to naively ask, "What is the traditional topping—if any—to use?"

CORNISH PASTIES

INGREDIENTS

Dough
1 cup all-purpose flour
Pinch of salt
1/2 stick butter
1/4 cup (4 tablespoons) shortening (original recipe called for lard)
Cold water to mix

Filling
8 ounces lean steak (sirloin, top round, filet)
1 small onion, finely chopped
1 potato, peeled and diced
1 turnip, peeled and diced
Salt/pepper
1 egg, beaten

PROCEDURE

Dough
- In mixing bowl, combine flour and salt.
- Blend butter and shortening into the flour until the mixture resembles fine bread crumbs.
- Add enough water to make a firm dough.
- Chill dough until needed.

Filling
- Cut steak into small thin strips and place in bowl with vegetables; salt/pepper to taste.
- Roll out chilled dough and cut out 6 circles about the size of a luncheon plate.
- Pile equal amounts of the meat/vegetable mixture in the center of each of the 6 dough circles.
- Dampen the edges with beaten egg.
- Fold the dough circles in half so that the edges meet; pinch together to seal.
- Place on lightly greased baking sheet and brush with beaten egg to glaze.
- Cut a small slit in the top of each pasty to allow steam to escape.
- Bake at 375 degrees for 20 to 35 minutes or until golden brown.

NOTES

This recipe came from a traditional British cookbook. Often times, pasties were made very large and had a thick rope-like edging on one side for the miner to use as a handle, thus preventing the rest of his meal from getting dirty. Initials were often marked on one corner so the pasty could be identified later if the miner didn't consume it at one sitting.

WELSH PASTIES

INGREDIENTS

Dough

3 cups all-purpose flour

1 tablespoon salt

1 cup shortening (original recipe called for lard)

1 cup cold water

Filling

3 and 3/4 cups potatoes, cubed

15 ounces (approximately) flank steak, cubed

5 ounces (approximately) pork, cubed

5 teaspoons shortening (The original recipe called for suet! Where does one buy that now?)

5 tablespoons onion, diced

Salt/pepper to taste

PROCEDURE

Dough

- Sift flour and salt into mixing bowl and sift second time.
- Cut in shortening until mixture is size of small peas.
- Add cold water, a little at a time.
- Toss until mixture holds together (handle as little as possible).
- Divide into 5 portions.
- Roll each portion on a floured board until about 9 inches across.

Filling

- Combine all filling ingredients.
- Pile equal amounts in the center of each of the 5 dough circles.
- Fold over, pinch the edges to seal, and make a slit on top to allow steam to escape.
- Place on greased baking sheet.
- Bake at 400 degrees for about 1 hour or until nicely browned.

NOTES

This recipe came from an old Wisconsin Welsh family whose name I've forgotten, but it is authentic.

PIES

Pie was not invented in Wisconsin, but pie as we know it today is certainly an American concoction. As immigrants knew, pie was a meal, like a steak-and-kidney pie. But in those days animals brought from Europe to America were too valuable to be slaughtered for meat; they were needed to till the fields, to breed so herds could be built, or to provide milk. Since fruit trees were so prolific in Pennsylvania Dutch country, a pie was filled with fruit rather than meat or vegetables. Perhaps at holiday time one animal might be slaughtered and divided up among many settlers to provide them with a good, large roast. Smaller scraps, innards, or tongue would be combined with apples, raisins, and spices to form the basics of a mincemeat pie.

The Amish brought to Wisconsin their pie-making skills, and many Amish homemakers today bake pies for restaurants. So if your waitress ever says to you, "We serve Amish pies—a local Amish lady makes them," don't pass up that piece of pie no matter how full you may be!

A bit of pie trivia: Pies were made round, rather than oblong or square, as a frugality measure, since it allowed colonial women to "cut corners" and stretch ingredients. Making a pie shallow also contributed to that end. As pies evolved into sweet treats, the expression "sweetie pie" became a term of endearment. Young men often referred to their homes as "the pie house" — a tribute to their mothers' baking skills.

Pie tips: It's easy to cut a pie into four or six or even eight pieces—but five? Here's how: From the center, cut a straight line to the edge; from the center above the line, cut a V. You now have a capital Y, the upper part making a wedge. Divide the two remaining large sections in half and you will have five pieces—all the same size. If you use a ceramic pie plate with an unglazed bottom your pie crust won't be soggy. The unglazed exterior allows the pan to breathe and retards the build-up of moisture.

MUERBE TEIG PIE CRUST

INGREDIENTS

1/4 cup butter
1 tablespoon sugar
1 egg yolk
1 cup flour

PROCEDURE

- Cream butter and sugar.
- Add egg yolk and a smidgen of salt.
- Add flour and mix.
- Press dough into greased pie plate and refrigerate overnight.
- When ready to bake pie, pour in filling and bake per pie instructions.

NOTES

The German words *muerbe teig* mean "delicate dough". This German family recipe was passed down from mother to daughter. The "daughter" I got it from is now in her seventies and one of the best cooks I know. My wife and I relish invitations to her house for dinner.

OLD-FASHIONED APPLE PIE

INGREDIENTS

Filling

3/4 cup sugar (use 1 cup if you don't plan to use the crumb topping)

2 tablespoons flour

1/2 to 1 teaspoon cinnamon

1/8 to 1/4 teaspoon nutmeg (I use freshly grated nutmeg, but it's not essential.)

1/4 teaspoon salt

7 cups apples (about 2 to 2 and 1/2 pounds), peeled and sliced

2 tablespoons butter

Crumbs

1/2 cup butter

1/2 cup light brown sugar, packed

1 cup flour

PROCEDURE

Filling

• Combine sugar, flour, cinnamon, nutmeg, and salt.

• Add apples and mix.

• Heap in a 9-inch unbaked pie shell.

• Dot top with butter.

Crumbs

• Combine all ingredients until crumbly and mixture makes little balls.

• Place crumbs on top of pie.

• Bake at 400 degrees for 45 to 55 minutes.

NOTES

This recipe was originally from the *1965 Complete Pie Cookbook* of the *Farm Journal* but I have made adjustments that must be for the best since everyone always raves about this apple pie. How much more American can one get than that? Since there are a lot of apples in this recipe, I use a deep-dish pie crust. The crumbs tend to get a little dark while baking, so towards the end I cover the top lightly with foil. The crumbs should be golden brown.

SOUR CREAM
PRUNE PIE

INGREDIENTS

Filling

3 egg yolks

1 cup sour cream

1 tablespoon vinegar

1 cup cooked prunes (chopped)

1 scant cup sugar

1/2 teaspoon each of cinnamon, cloves, nutmeg, and salt

Meringue

3 egg whites

5 tablespoons sugar

PROCEDURE

Filling

- Combine all ingredients.
- Pour into unbaked crust.
- Bake at 350 degrees for 30 minutes.
- Cool.

Meringue

- Beat egg whites and slowly add the sugar.
- Place meringue on top of cooled pie.
- Bake at 250 degrees until meringue is golden brown.

NOTES

I do like prunes, and all the spices give this recipe an excellent flavor.

MINCEMEAT PIE

INGREDIENTS

2 cups ground chuck, browned

3 cups apples, ground

1/2 cup brown sugar

1/4 teaspoon salt

1 teaspoon cinnamon

1/2 teaspoon cloves

2 tablespoons whiskey or bourbon (maybe more?)

4 tablespoons black cherry wine (if you don't have any, leave it out)

Raisins, optional but a handful or two makes the pie better

1 9-inch two-crust pie crust, unbaked

PROCEDURE

- Combine meat, apples, sugar, salt, and spices in saucepan.
- Cook over low heat until thoroughly heated. If mixture seems to be getting too dry add a little beef broth.
- Stir in whiskey, wine, and raisins.
- Pour mixture into unbaked pie shell, cover with top crust, seal edges.
- Bake at 350 degrees for 45 minutes.

NOTES

One can buy ready-made mincemeat in cans or jars, but be sure to compare the ingredients. The more expensive one contains "the good stuff" and is well worth the additional cost.

EASY SHOO-FLY PIE

INGREDIENTS

1 cup brown sugar

1 cup all-purpose flour

1 scant teaspoon baking soda

2 tablespoons vegetable oil

1 cup molasses

1 cup warm water

1 beaten egg

1 teaspoon vanilla

PROCEDURE

- Combine all ingredients and mix well.
- Pour into an unbaked pie shell.
- Bake at 350 degrees for 35 minutes or until toothpick or cake tester comes out clean.

NOTES

This is an authentic Amish recipe, and the gentleman who provided it says the mixture will develop its own topping while baking. Most Shoo-Fly Pie recipes, however, call for a separate crumb topping. There are two versions for the source of the name Shoo-Fly. One says the pie was baked to draw flies from other foods in the kitchen or from the milk and butter in the springhouse, and this pie was never meant to be eaten. The other version says it merely referred to the need to shoo away flies while this sweet dessert was cooling (remember, way back when, there were no window screens).

BOURBON PECAN PIE

INGREDIENTS

1 stick of butter, cut into 1/2-inch cubes

1 cup sugar

1 cup white corn syrup

4 eggs

1 tablespoon bourbon

1/2 cup chocolate chips

1 cup chopped pecans

1 unbaked pie shell

PROCEDURE

- Combine all ingredients.
- Pour into pie shell.
- Bake at 350 degrees for 45 minutes.

NOTES

To prevent spills in the oven, you may want to put foil or a cookie sheet under the pie plate. Many years ago while working on a governors' cookbook project, I received this recipe from Martha Layne Collins, governor of Kentucky from 1979 through 1987. She served this dessert in the executive mansion. Coming from Kentucky, is it any wonder that bourbon is a part of this recipe?

LEFSE

When he isn't plundering, sacking, or pillaging, the comic strip character Hagar the Horrible pronounces that "feasting is a major Viking pastime." Wife Helga keeps him well fed on sardines and a whole array of other Norwegian fish. Wisconsin Norwegians continue to be partial to fish of all sorts. But they also have a mutton and cabbage stew that has acquired the status of a national favorite. The Norwegian food probably most familiar to everyone is lefse. It can refer to the Norwegian pancake or to a flatbread sometimes made with potato. Lefse flatbreads are of two kinds. One is a soft, fresh-served variety, while the other is a hard version that is moistened before serving.

LEFSE

INGREDIENTS

10 cups mashed potatoes
1 stick butter, melted
1 tablespoon sugar (helps make the lefse brown)
1 tablespoon baking powder
1/4 teaspoon salt
1/2 cup heavy cream
4 to 5 cups flour

PROCEDURE

- In large bowl, combine potatoes with butter, sugar, baking powder, salt, and cream; blend well.
- Cool slightly and add just enough flour to handle.
- Add additional flour slowly until the dough is similar in consistency to pie crust dough.
- Cool completely at room temperature and roll mixture very thin on lightly floured surface in 8- to 9-inch circles.
- To prevent sticking, dough must be rolled with a covered rolling pin or specially ridged rolling pin (lefse rolling pin).
- Bake dough on a lefse grill or pancake grill, turning only once when the underside is brown spotted.
- To serve, cut dough into pie-shaped wedges, butter, and roll up.

NOTES

Lefse pieces were traditionally wrapped around a piece of fish or meat to make eating less messy. Sounds like the original Norwegian sandwich. Rolling pin covers or lefse rolling pins are available at kitchen specialty stores.

EAST WISCONSIN WATERS
CHAPTER THREE

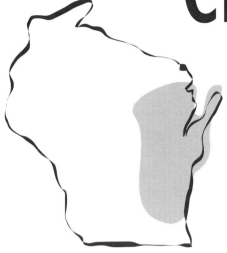

BROWN

CALUMET

DOOR

FOND DU LAC

GREEN LAKE

KEWAUNEE

MANITOWOC

MENOMINEE

OUTAGAMIE

SHAWANO

SHEBOYGAN

WAUPACA

WAUSHARA

WINNEBAGO

Although the Indian Packing Company canned its last vegetables and went out of business years ago, it left a lasting legacy—the Green Bay Packers! To help the team get started in 1919, the company provided the athletic field, the jerseys, and the name. This part of Wisconsin has made at least two other contributions to American culture and cuisine as well.

The ice cream sundae was invented in Two Rivers in Manitowoc County. One day in 1881, George Hallaver strolled into Edward Berner's ice cream parlor and asked Berner to put chocolate sauce *on top* of his five-cent dish of ice cream. Until then Berner had put chocolate sauce only in ice cream sodas. The deed was done and it was an instant hit. Charles Giffey, a confectioner in neighboring Manitowoc, feared that Berner's inexpensive and popular invention would hurt his business and convinced him to serve the concoction only on Sunday. Berner complied, until a ten-year-old girl asked for the Sunday dish on a weekday. What the heck, thought Berner, let's serve Sundays every day. Business is business! A glassware salesman (with a spelling problem) coined the word *sundae* when he ordered the canoe-shaped dishes in which the Sunday was served.

Another American classic, the hamburger, was invented in Seymour, in Outagamie County. In 1885 Charlie Nagreen was selling meatballs at the county fair, an item his customers found awkward to eat while walking around the fair. He flattened the meatballs, put them between two pieces of bread, and the hamburger was born. Now, where would all of today's fast food chains be if it weren't for the ingenious Charlie?

But in Wisconsin, hamburgers are second to bratwurst when it comes to the cookout. Sheboygan is known as the Wurst City in the World, and it seems that every little neighborhood grocery has its own recipe for making bratwurst. This delectable German pork sausage is generally referred to simply as *brats* (pronounced *brahts* to distinguish it from the word for naughty kids).

Brats are generally cooked over an outside grill of charcoal or briquettes, a process affectionately referred to as a fry—one fries out in summer. The traditional method is to place the uncooked sausage on a grill, keep the fire hot but not flaming, and to douse any flare-up with a squirt from a clean plastic ketchup bottle of water (aimed at the coals, not at the brats!). The sausage should be turned often until done to ensure thorough cooking—a good fryer knows when that is. Slight finger pressure on the sausage will indicate whether the sausage is firm, a good clue that they are done. Brats should be golden brown, not charred black.

Over the years bratwurst frying has almost achieved haute cuisine status with as many expert opinions on to how to prepare it (marinated in combinations of beer, onions, mustards) as where to buy it. Some brats are coarsely ground, some quite spicy. Even the kind of roll to serve them on is a matter of discussion and dispute. One really needs a good "hard" roll—soft inside but crusty outside.

As further proof of its meat credentials, Wisconsin is the largest producer of veal in the nation. Aat Groenevelt of Holland introduced the Dutch method of producing specially fed veal when he opened a calf feed plant in New Jersey in 1962 and located its first packing facility in Seymour, Wisconsin, in 1974. While veal is almost commonplace in Europe, it is a relatively recent commercial venture in this country.

Wisconsin is the fourth largest producer of maple syrup in the country. According to Wisconsin Chippewa legend, the spirit of Man-a-bo-zho brought the gift of sugar to the Great Lakes region. With tomahawks the Chippewa made slices in the trees and inserted twigs to direct the sap into baskets. Today Wisconsin's three thousand producers annually turn out over 110,000 gallons of syrup—a staggering amount, since it takes about forty gallons of raw syrup to make just one gallon of the final product. Weather is a crucial factor in maple syrup production, and its unpredictability contributes to the final cost of maple syrup. No wonder it's called liquid gold! But the taste is well worth whatever it costs. The area around the small town of Aniwa in Shawano County produces much of the world's maple syrup.

Cruising around the Door County peninsula (between Lake Michigan on its east and the bay of Green Bay on its west), one feasts upon 250 miles of picturesque shoreline. The scenery is particularly beautiful when the four thousand acres of cherry and apple trees blossom. Wisconsin ranks sixth in the production of tart cherries, 98 percent of which grow on more than a million trees in Door County.

Surrounded by water, Door County residents enjoy fish, especially the fish boil. Willie Johnson, who lived to ninety-seven, loved to tell the tale of getting caught on the ice one December. Seems the ice shifted and he was stranded for seven days with only potatoes, salt, and the fish he had caught. But on his boat he happened to have a kettle, a stove, and plenty of wood. He cooked it all up and created the first fish boil. Bill Beckstrom, a state park employee, heard the story and invited campers to join him at his campfire for boiled fish. Cliff Wenniger, a commercial fisherman with ten boats, invited workers and their families to a fish boil after the spring run of whitefish. From that time on, the fish boil was a recognized regional dish. The first commercial fish boil was sponsored by the Fish Creek Community Church in the summer of 1947. Laurence Wickman, owner of the Viking Restaurant, had a few "boils" for tourists, and they grew so popular that when he died in 1973 his tombstone read Founder of the Viking Fish Boil.

Naturally there's a food story behind the name of the little Door County town of Egg Harbor. In the mid-1800s a popular Sunday pastime was to row along the Green Bay shore. On one such Sunday, two boats full of frisky tourists started throwing eggs at one another (for some reason lost to history), and the litter of shells on the beach after the battle inspired the name Egg Harbor. And that is a historical food fact!

SAUSAGE

Sausage has been known around the world for at least three thousand years. The word comes from the Latin *salsus* ("salted"). Wurstmachers (sausage makers) from Germany, Austria, Switzerland, and Poland set up shop in Wisconsin, and all of them had brought their prized old-world recipes with them.

The tradition lives on, for Wisconsin produces well over 450 million pounds of fresh, cooked, or dried sausages per year. It ranks third in the nation, and it is said that Wisconsin's Wurst is America's Best.

Many sausage manufacturers retain the original methods of production, smoking the sausages slowly over smoldering hardwood slabs and sawdust to provide a natural smoke flavor, rather than using liquid smoke. They will use only natural spices and fresh garlic or onions, rather than powdered or flake substitutes. A good sausage will contain no fillers such as milk, powder, or cereals, and some sausage makers are proud to say their sausage needs no such flavor enhancers as MSG (monosodium glutamate).

Choice of sausage is a matter of taste and occasion. A Wisconsin-style supper might have ring or straight bologna—same ingredients, different shape. Both are fully cooked and need only to be reheated—never boil them or the casing will burst. There is also a good variety of breakfast sausages in either patty or link form. But my favorite breakfast meat is Canadian bacon. It's cut from the loin along the pig's back and is a lean, drier, and fully cooked meat. How it came to be called Canadian bacon is unclear—in Canada it is called back bacon. Eggs Benedict, of course, is a favorite way to enjoy Canadian bacon. For a snack or as an excellent appetizer with crackers, try any one of the hundreds of summer sausages (soft or hard) or salami, and take your choice of the all-beef kind, the pork and beef combo, with garlic or without. For sandwiches there are olive loaf, pickle and pimento loaf—again, a great range of varieties. And every sausage lover is thoroughly acquainted with braunschweiger, Polish kielbasa, Mettwurst, and bockwurst. Many hunters, fishermen, and campers pack landjaeger—a firm Swiss dried beef stick that needs no refrigeration, so it's an excellent snack for outdoor energy.

Bratwurst is one of Wisconsin's most famous sausages. On almost any summer day one can whiff that delicious aroma and know that someone in the neighborhood is frying brats. Every weekend some civic group or other has a fry to raise money. Most brats come fresh and need to be thoroughly cooked; precooked brats need only to be heated. While there used to be only one combination of ingredients (beef and pork), now brats come in a many flavors: jalapeno, Cajun, wine, beer, no-salt, garlic, and so on.

Since the Jaycees of Sheboygan held its first annual Bratwurst Day in 1953, the city has become the Bratwurst Capitol of the World. In 1997 Sheboygan sold about 4,500 pounds of brats, the equivalent of 22,500 bratwurst sandwiches. For an international flavor they introduced "Bratxotic," whereby local restaurants serve exotic brat concoctions with their particular ethnic flavor—brat pizza, brat taco, brat gyros, and brat fleisbrot.

BUTTER-SIMMERED ONIONS

INGREDIENTS

4 to 6 medium onions, sliced into rings
1/2 to1 stick butter

PROCEDURE

- Melt butter in a heavy 10- to 12-inch skillet.
- Place onion rings in melted butter and cover.
- Simmer at medium heat for about one hour.
- Reduce heat to low and allow to simmer at least 2 more hours, stirring occasionally.
- Keep covered the entire time since the onions will generate their own juice.
- Toward the end of the cooking time, the onions should be limp and yellowish, and cover may be removed to reduce some of the moisture, making the onions even more golden brown.
- Allow to simmer uncovered about 20 minutes more.
- May be served immediately or left to cool and then reheated when ready to use.

NOTES

These onions are superb on a bratwurst sandwich. They also add a new dimension to an ordinary hamburger sandwich. The onions reduce to a third or a fourth of the original quantity.

BRATWURST HORS D'OEUVRES

INGREDIENTS

3 pounds uncooked bratwurst, cut into 1/2-inch slices

1 can (28 ounces) sauerkraut (do not drain)

1/2 cup brown sugar

PROCEDURE

- Sauté bratwurst slices (they do not have to be cooked thoroughly at this point).
- Drain off any grease.
- Add sauerkraut with its juice.
- Let mixture sit a couple of hours—overnight is best.
- Add sugar and simmer 4 to 6 hours.
- Serve in chafing dish with toothpicks.

NOTES

I was first served this at a pontoon boat picnic—a dozen or more people with pontoon boats lash the boats together in the middle of the lake and walk from boat to boat drinking, eating, and socializing. Really fun!

PICKLED BOLOGNA HORS D'OEUVRES

INGREDIENTS

1 pound ring or straight bologna, skinned, and cut into 1/2-inch slices

1 and 1/2 cups water

2 tablespoons sugar

1 and 1/2 teaspoons salt

20 peppercorns

16 whole allspice

1 jar (7 ounces) roasted peppers

1 medium onion, sliced

PROCEDURE

- Combine water, sugar, salt, peppercorns, and allspice and bring to a boil.
- Reduce heat, cover, and simmer 10 minutes.
- Remove from heat and cool.
- Layer bologna slices on bottom of casserole.
- Cover with onion and roasted peppers.
- Pour liquid over the top.
- Cover and chill at least 3 days.
- To serve: Remove bologna slices from liquid and serve with toothpicks or on crackers.

FULL OF BOLOGNA CASSEROLE

INGREDIENTS

1 and 1/2 cups bologna, skinned and cubed

1 and 1/2 cups raw potatoes, cubed

1 can cream of celery soup

2 large slices cheese (cheddar or Swiss), quartered

PROCEDURE

- Mix bologna, potatoes, and soup in 1 and 1/2-quart baking dish.
- Bake covered at 350 degrees for 1 hour.
- Remove cover, top with cheese, and broil until cheese is bubbly and brown.

NOTES

This recipe came from the *Country Favorites* cookbook of the Wisconsin Bird and Game Breeders Association. I don't know the connection between that organization and bologna. Was one of their members trying to make a statement?

HOT DOGS WITH ORIGINAL CONEY ISLAND SAUCE

INGREDIENTS

1 pound ground chuck
1 medium onion, chopped
3 tablespoons chili powder
1 teaspoon salt
3/4 teaspoon dried oregano
3/4 teaspoon cumin powder
1/4 teaspoon red pepper flakes
2 cups water
1 small can tomato sauce (optional)
Grated cheddar cheese (optional)

PROCEDURE

- Brown meat and onions.
- Drain any grease.
- Add next five ingredients and mix well.
- Add water and simmer for I hour.
- Tomato sauce may be added to the mixture before serving, if desired.
- To serve: Spoon mixture over hot dog in bun and top with grated cheese.

NOTES

The original Coney Island hot dogs were served without sauce. They became so popular that New Yorkers started calling all hot dogs Coney Islands. As their popularity spread throughout the rest of the country, Coney Island hot dogs acquired a variety of condiments. This is the authentic recipe for the sauce.

OVEN-BARBECUED HOT DOGS

INGREDIENTS

1 package (8 to 10) hot dogs

1 medium onion, finely diced

2 tablespoons butter

2 tablespoons vinegar

2 tablespoons brown sugar

4 tablespoons lemon juice

1 cup ketchup

3 tablespoons Worcestershire sauce

1/2 tablespoon prepared mustard

1/2 cup water

1/2 cup celery, chopped

PROCEDURE

- Brown onions in butter.
- Add remaining ingredients and simmer 30 minutes.
- Prick skins of hot dogs and arrange in shallow pan; pour barbecue sauce over the top.
- Bake uncovered at 350 degrees for 45 minutes.

NOTES

The wife of a major Milwaukee sausage manufacturer provided this recipe for the *Visiting Nurse Association Cookbook* in 1938.

REUBEN SAUSAGE CASSEROLE

INGREDIENTS

1 package "lite" breakfast sausage links

10 slices rye bread, cubed

1 small can (4 ounces) sauerkraut, drained and rinsed

2 cups low-fat shredded cheese, such as mozzarella

6 eggs lightly beaten or equivalent egg substitute

3 cups skim milk

1/4 teaspoon pepper

PROCEDURE

- Brown sausage over low heat, drain any grease, and cool slightly.
- Cut sausage crosswise into coin-size pieces.
- Lightly butter (or spray) a 9 x 13 baking dish.
- Arrange bread cubes on the bottom.
- Cover bread with sausage, sauerkraut, and shredded cheese.
- Mix together eggs, milk, and pepper until well blended.
- Pour mixture over sausage.
- Cover and refrigerate overnight.
- Bake covered at 350 degrees for 45 minutes.
- Uncover and bake 10 more minutes until puffed and bubbly.

NOTES

Serves 10 easily.

KIELBASA PASTA SALAD

INGREDIENTS

12 ounces Polish kielbasa sausage

1 and 1/2 cups large (1-inch) shell macaroni

6 slices bacon, diced

1 cup fresh mushrooms, sliced

3 tablespoons sugar

2 tablespoons all-purpose flour

1/2 teaspoon salt

1/8 teaspoon pepper

1 and 1/4 cups water (divided into 1/2 cup and 3/4 cup)

1/2 cup tarragon vinegar

2 tablespoons parsley, snipped

PROCEDURE

- Place sausage and 1/2 cup water into skillet, cover, and simmer for about 20 minutes.
- Cook macaroni according to package directions and drain.
- Drain and slice sausage and set aside.
- In large skillet fry bacon until crisp and drain; reserve about 3 tablespoons drippings in the skillet.
- Cook mushrooms in the drippings for about 2 minutes.
- Stir in sugar, flour, salt, and pepper.
- Add 3/4 cup water and vinegar.
- Cook and stir until thickened and bubbly.
- Add sausage, macaroni, bacon, and parsley.
- Toss together lightly and serve.
- Additional parsley may be added for garnish.

NOTES

Serves 4 to 6. Other sausages may be used, but the special kielbasa sausage flavor makes this salad what it is.

SAUSAGE TOSTADO SALAD

INGREDIENTS

1 package (8 ounces) beef sausages, chopped

1 can (15 ounces) chili beans, undrained

1/2 of a 1 and 1/4-ounce package of taco seasoning mix

4 crisp tostado shells

3 cups shredded lettuce

1 cup shredded cheese (Monterey Jack)

2 medium tomatoes, chopped

1/4 cup black olives, sliced

Guacamole or sour cream for garnish

PROCEDURE

- Place chopped links in 1 and 1/2-quart casserole.
- Microwave at 50% for 4 minutes.
- Add taco seasoning and undrained beans.
- Cover and microwave at 100% for 2 to 3 minutes, stirring at least once.
- Place each tostado shell on plate and layer with lettuce, sausage mixture, cheese, tomatoes, and olives.
- Serve with guacamole or sour cream.

NOTES

I thought this book should contain at least one microwave recipe.

MAPLE-GLAZED BREAKFAST SAUSAGE

INGREDIENTS

2 8-ounce packages brown-and-serve or pork link sausages, unflavored
1/2 cup maple syrup
1/4 cup firmly packed brown sugar
l teaspoon cinnamon

PROCEDURE

- In large skillet, brown sausages and drain.
- In small bowl, combine syrup, sugar, and cinnamon and blend well.
- Pour over sausages until well coated; heat thoroughly, stirring gently.

NOTES

Even though this is a simple recipe, the smell is tremendously appealing, and the maple taste makes a breakfast of scrambled eggs or pancakes a gourmet experience.

VEAL

Where would the Italians be without veal scaloppini or the Germans without Wiener schnitzel? Certainly, Wisconsin is making sure these culinary masterpieces will continue to be served. It ranks first in the nation for special-fed veal calves, producing 195,000 head per year, and one of the finest producers is the Provimi Company in the Fox River Valley and Green Bay area (Brown County). It derived its name from the words *proteins*, *vitamins* and *minerals*—the basic components of animal feed.

Veal lacks fat. It is tender, but its connective tissue requires veal cuts to be cooked slowly unless sliced or pounded. Wisconsin's special-fed veal is as close as one can come to a natural organic meat. The type of feeding is called milk-fed or fancy versus the lower quality grain-fed or bob veal (newborn calves).

It's a little surprising that veal is not as popular as turkey, perhaps because veal is relatively expensive compared with turkey. A half-ounce serving of veal has three grams of protein, only fifteen calories, and no fat or cholesterol. It definitely is a heart-healthy meat.

Veal comes in a variety of cuts: roasts, chops, slices, patties, cube steaks, or ground. My best meat loaf recipe calls for ground chuck with smaller portions of ground pork and ground veal. The addition of the veal and pork boosts the meat loaf from the good category to the excellent category. I add finely minced onion, shredded carrot, some ketchup, bread crumbs, and salt and pepper.

Veal has been esteemed as a delicate meat since biblical times but it achieved its greatest popularity in Italy. It is still popular in Italian and French restaurants, but you should really try making it at home.

VEAL SCALOPPINI

INGREDIENTS

12 veal steaks, thinly sliced

8 tablespoons butter (divided into 5 and 3 tablespoons)

3/4 cup mushrooms, sliced

1 small onion, finely chopped

1 clove garlic

3 cups tomatoes

2/3 cup dry white wine

1/4 teaspoon tarragon

Romano cheese, grated

PROCEDURE

- Melt 5 tablespoons butter.
- Sauté mushrooms for 5 minutes.
- Add onions and garlic; sauté until golden brown.
- Add tomatoes, wine, and tarragon and stir until blended.
- Simmer covered for 30 minutes.
- In 3 tablespoons butter, gently fry veal pieces.
- Add to sauce and simmer 5 minutes.
- Serve and sprinkle grated cheese on top of each veal piece.

NOTES

This is a family recipe from my nephew's wife, who has an Italian background.

WIENER SCHNITZEL

INGREDIENTS

1 to 2 pounds thinly sliced veal

3 eggs

1/4 cup cold milk

1/4 teaspoon salt

1/4 teaspoon white pepper

2 cups bread crumbs, finely crushed

1 onion, medium to large, sliced

4 to 6 tablespoons butter

PROCEDURE

- In shallow pie plate or cake pan, mix eggs, milk, salt, and pepper.
- Put bread crumbs into another shallow pan.
- Dip serving size veal pieces into egg/milk mixture and then into bread crumbs, coating both sides.
- Set coated veal pieces aside on wax paper and allow to rest for 5 to 10 minutes.
- Dip the pieces a second time in the egg/milk mixture and then into bread crumbs.
- Let veal rest for another 5 to 10 minutes.
- Melt butter in heavy skillet and sauté onions until limp.
- Remove onions to a holding dish.
- Brown the veal pieces approximately 5 to 7 minutes on each side, being careful when turning not to remove the breading.
- Return sautéed onions to same skillet with veal and simmer covered for an additional 3 to 5 minutes to warm the onions.

NOTES

This is my wife's recipe. I never order schnitzel, even at a German restaurant, because no one can equal hers! The secret to retaining the bread crumb coating is the resting period and the second coating.

VEAL LOAF

INGREDIENTS

3 pounds ground veal

2 cups minced onion

2 cups minced celery

2 tablespoons lemon rind

1 and 1/2 teaspoons allspice

3 tablespoons fresh chopped dill, OR 1 and 1/2 tablespoons dried crushed dill

2 cups bread crumbs

1 and 1/2 cups sour cream

3 eggs

16 hard-cooked eggs, peeled (do not slice)

PROCEDURE

- Combine all ingredients except hard-cooked eggs.
- Spray or oil four 8-1/2 x 4-1/2 loaf pans.
- Fill each pan to 1/3 with the veal mixture.
- Place the whole hard-cooked eggs in a row down the center.
- Fill with remainder of veal mixture.
- Cover pans with foil and bake at 350 degrees for 30 minutes.
- Remove foil and bake another 20 minutes.
- Cool slightly before slicing with a sharp knife.

NOTES

These four loaves provide 24 servings, so if you don't need that much, just scale down the recipe. The circle of hard-cooked egg in the center of each slice of veal loaf provides a novel appearance.

VEAL STEW

INGREDIENTS

1 cup flour

2 teaspoons salt

2 teaspoons pepper

7 pounds of veal for stewing (1-inch cubes)

1/2 cup olive oil

10 large coarsely chopped onions (yes, they do boil down)

3 tablespoons minced garlic

2 tablespoons dried thyme leaves

1 and 1/4 quarts chicken broth (use a chicken soup base if you prefer)

3 pounds baby carrots

3 pounds small new red potatoes, halved or quartered

3 cups frozen peas

1/4 cup minced fresh thyme OR a scant 1/8 cup dried thyme

PROCEDURE

- In large bowl, combine flour, salt, and pepper.
- Add veal and toss to coat.
- Brown veal cubes evenly in hot oil.
- Remove from skillet and set aside.
- To same skillet, add onion, garlic, and thyme and sauté 3 to 4 minutes.
- Return veal cubes to pan.
- Stir in chicken broth.
- Bring to a boil, reduce heat, cover tightly, and simmer 45 minutes.
- Add carrots and potatoes, cover, and continue to cook another 30 minutes.
- Skim fat from cooking liquid, if necessary.
- Stir in peas and cook until heated (about 3 to 4 minutes), stirring occasionally.
- To serve, ladle portions into serving bowls and sprinkle with thyme.

NOTES

The quantities may seem large, but the recipe makes only 12 servings. Still too much? Invite some guests, or enjoy the leftovers in the next few days. Vary the dish by serving with baking powder biscuits or over pasta or rice.

MAPLE SYRUP

Wisconsin's state tree is the sugar maple. In autumn its leaves are glorious shades of red and gold. One just feels the tree is soaking up all the sunshine it can so that in spring when it is tapped it can produce a gush of its "sweetwater" to be turned into maple syrup. Good syrup production requires a sunny thirty to forty degrees during the day and a brisk twenty-five degrees at night. According to an old farmer's adage, "When the wind is from the East, the sap will run the least. When the wind is from the West, the sap will run the best."

After the sap is gathered it has to be cooked to evaporate the water in the shortest time in order to produce a lighter colored and more delicately flavored syrup. The process is called "sugaring."

Maple syrup is a natural sweetener, free of additives. It is sweeter than sugar and adds extra moisture to a recipe. The Wisconsin Maple Syrup Producers Council recommends substituting maple syrup for sugar as follows: Use one and a half cups of maple syrup for each cup of granulated sugar. Add one-fourth teaspoon baking soda for each cup of maple syrup. When substituting maple syrup for all the sugar in a recipe, decrease the liquid by one half. For example, if a recipe calls for one cup sugar and a half cup of milk, you may substitute one and a half cups maple syrup, plus one-fourth teaspoon baking soda, and reduce the milk to one-fourth cup. Remember also

that maple syrup adds a brownish tinge to whatever you are making and tends to make baked goods brown more quickly than if white sugar were used.

No doubt about it, pure maple syrup is expensive but well worth it, depending on how you use it. It is graded Fancy (the finest), Grades A and B, and Unclassified, which is often a blend of maple syrup and sugar cane syrup. A, B, and Unclassified are often called pancake syrups. P. J. Towle of Saint Paul, Minnesota, introduced this kind of blend in 1887 under the name Log Cabin syrup and packaged it in a tin shaped like the kind of cabin his hero Abraham Lincoln lived in. If you want the genuine maple syrup, always look for the words "Pure Maple Syrup."

I'm fortunate to have a maple syrup farm just about two miles from my house. It has about two thousand trees spread over a hundred acres and taps some trees by hanging pails on the trees to collect the sap. The more modern way is to connect the trees to the syrup house with plastic tubing. There the "sugaring" takes place—from sap to syrup, from vat to bottle.

Maple syrup in sealed containers keeps well at room temperature. Once opened, it should be stored in the refrigerator. If mold develops, skim it off and boil the syrup a few minutes. If a sugary crust or crystals form, dissolve them simply by setting the container in a pan of hot water.

MAPLE GRANOLA

INGREDIENTS

4 cups oatmeal

1 cup coconut

1 cup chopped nuts (your favorite kind)

1/2 cup whole bran cereal

1/2 cup toasted sesame seeds

1/2 teaspoon salt (optional)

1/2 cup vegetable oil

1/2 cup maple syrup

PROCEDURE

- In a large bowl, combine all dry ingredients.
- Add oil and maple syrup and stir to combine and coat dry ingredients.
- Spread mixture in jelly roll pan or on cookie sheet with 4 sides (so mixture won't fall off when stirring).
- Bake at 325 degrees until crisp (about 20 to 30 minutes).
- Stir every 10 minutes.
- Cool on paper toweling.
- Store in airtight container.

NOTES

In addition to being a nice pop-in-the-mouth-snack, this granola is great over breakfast food and even better over ice cream or fruit.

DIETER'S MAPLE POWER SHAKE

INGREDIENTS

1 banana cut in chunks

1/4 cup maple syrup

1/2 cup vanilla ice milk, OR 1 cup frozen vanilla yogurt

1 orange in sections

6 ounces vanilla yogurt

PROCEDURE

- Put all ingredients in food processor or blender.
- Mix 1 minute and serve.

NOTES

Almost any fruit can be added or substituted, but bananas and oranges work best. This recipe is from the Wisconsin Maple Producers Council.

EASY MAPLE NUT BREAD

INGREDIENTS

1/2 cup sugar

1 egg

1 and 1/4 cups milk

3 cups prepared biscuit mix

1 cup chopped walnuts (I prefer pecans)

1/2 cup maple syrup

PROCEDURE

- Several hours before making the bread, add nuts to maple syrup and let stand or soak overnight in the refrigerator.
- In a large bowl, combine sugar, egg, milk, and biscuit mix.
- Beat at high speed for 30 seconds.
- Stir in nut mixture and pour into 2 well-greased loaf pans.
- Bake at 350 degrees for 1 hour.
- Cool before slicing.

NOTES

Another good recipe, compliments of the Wisconsin Maple Producers Council.

MAPLE WHIPPED BUTTER

INGREDIENTS

1/4 teaspoon plain gelatin

1 teaspoon cold water

1 cup (2 sticks) butter, softened

1 and 1/4 cups maple syrup

PROCEDURE

- In a small pan, sprinkle gelatin over the cold water.
- On low heat, stir until gelatin is dissolved.
- Allow gelatin to cool slightly.
- Whip butter with electric mixer until fluffy.
- Slowly add maple syrup to butter.
- Add cooled gelatin to butter.
- Mix until thoroughly combined.
- Keep refrigerated until ready to use.

NOTES

This recipe makes about two cups. Spread on bread; great on pancakes or French toast. Another recipe from the Wisconsin Maple Producers Council.

MAPLE COPYCAT (KIT-KAT) BARS

INGREDIENTS

1 cup (2 sticks) butter
1/2 cup milk
1 cup maple syrup
2 cups graham cracker crumbs
1/2 cup brown sugar
Saltine crackers

PROCEDURE

- Line a 9 x 13-inch pan with saltine crackers.
- Heat butter and milk until butter is melted.
- Add maple syrup, graham cracker crumbs, and brown sugar.
- Boil for 5 minutes stirring continuously.
- Pour 1/2 of the cooked mixture over the saltine crackers.
- Place another layer of crackers over that.
- Pour remaining cooked mixture over that layer.
- Finish with another layer of crackers.
- Chill.

NOTES

The Wisconsin Maple Syrup Producers Council says this recipe may not put the Kit-Kat candy bar folks out of business, but it's fun for kids to make at home and snack on after school.

MAPLE SYRUP APPLE CAKE

INGREDIENTS

1 and 1/2 sticks butter, softened

1/2 cup brown sugar

1/2 cup oatmeal

2 cups all-purpose flour

2 quarts apples, sliced

1 and 1/2 cups maple syrup

2 tablespoons cornstarch

1 and 1/2 teaspoons vanilla

Whipped cream

PROCEDURE

- Mix butter, sugar, oatmeal, and flour.
- Pour 3/4 of the mixture into bottom of a 9 x 13 pan.
- Place apple slices on top of mixture.
- In medium saucepan, combine maple syrup and cornstarch.
- Cook until thick.
- Add vanilla.
- Pour mixture over apple slices.
- Sprinkle on the remaining 1/4 of the original mixture.
- Bake at 350 degrees for 1 hour.
- Cool and serve with whipped cream.

NOTES

A Wisconsin Maple Syrup Producers Council recipe.

MAPLE SYRUP
DIP/TOPPING

INGREDIENTS

1 cup (8 ounces) cottage cheese
1 tablespoon mayonnaise
4 tablespoons maple syrup

PROCEDURE

- Blend until smooth.

NOTES

Especially good over a fruit salad.

MAPLE PECAN PIE

INGREDIENTS

1 pie shell, unbaked

1/4 cup butter

2/3 cup brown sugar, firmly packed

1/8 teaspoon salt

3/4 cup maple syrup

3 eggs, beaten until light

1 cup pecan pieces

1 teaspoon vanilla

PROCEDURE

- Cream butter, sugar, and salt.
- Stir in other ingredients.
- Pour into pie crust.
- Bake at 450 degrees for 10 minutes.
- Reduce heat to 350 degrees and bake 30 to 35 minutes longer.
- Cool and serve with whipped cream or a scoop of vanilla ice cream.

NOTES

This recipe came from one of the largest maple syrup producers in Wisconsin near the small town of Aniwa.

MAPLE FUDGE

INGREDIENTS

1 cup sugar

2 cups maple syrup

1/4 cup white syrup

1/2 cup milk or cream

1 tablespoon flour

1 tablespoon butter

PROCEDURE

- Mix all ingredients except butter.
- Cook to 232 degrees (you'll need a candy thermometer).
- Add butter.
- Cool and beat.
- Pour into small square cake pan.

NOTES

Who says fudge can be made only with chocolate?

CHERRIES

February is National Cherry Month but in Wisconsin late July is cherry time. Door County picks approximately 6.1 million pounds of tart red cherries then, mostly the Montmorency variety. These are now categorized as "tart" rather than "sour" and certainly can be eaten directly from the tree. The cherries haven't changed, but the word *sour* seemed to indicate that a pucker was inevitable.

Cherries originated in Asia and were eventually dispersed throughout Europe. American colonists found wild cherry trees, cultivated them, and crossbred them with European varieties. French colonists planted French cherry pits along the Saint Lawrence River and the Great Lakes. Door County provided ideal conditions.

Fresh cherries should be refrigerated immediately and kept away from produce with strong odors. Be careful not to get them wet before storing. When you do use them, it is helpful first to chill the cherries in very cold water for two to three hours (maximum). Chilling allows the fruit to firm, so it won't fall apart when pitted. You don't need a cherry pitter—just use a hairpin, paper clip, kitchen fork, or plastic straw. Bleach or lemon juice works well to remove any dark stains from your hands.

Nearly all the crop is processed as frozen or dried. Frozen cherries can be used in many recipes, especially those calling for fresh cherries, but you will need to know whether you're using sweetened or unsweetened cherries. Simply thaw, drain, and use. The juice may be used as a water substitute in cooking or as a pure, tasty drink.

Dried cherries came into existence in 1987 in the small town of Forestville (smack in the center of Door County) when a fledgling company called Country Ovens started dehydrating fresh Door County cherries. The dried fruit makes an excellent snack on its own but may also be used in any recipe calling for raisins.

DOOR COUNTY CHERRY COBBLER

INGREDIENTS

1 can (15 ounces) cherry pie filling

1/2 cup chopped nuts (your choice of walnuts or pecans)

1/3 cup (5 to 6 tablespoons) butter, softened

1/4 cup brown sugar

1 cup all-purpose flour, sifted

1 teaspoon cinnamon

PROCEDURE

- Pour cherry pie filling into a buttered baking dish.
- Sprinkle nuts on top.
- Blend butter, sugar, flour, and cinnamon until crumbly.
- Sprinkle mixture over top of pie filling.
- Bake at 400 degrees for 20 minutes.
- Cool.
- Serve with ice cream or whipped cream.

CHERRY TORTE

INGREDIENTS

Crust
1 cup graham cracker crumbs
1/2 cup sugar
1/2 cup (1 stick) butter, softened

Custard
3 cups milk
3 egg yolks, slightly beaten
3 tablespoons cornstarch
3/4 cup sugar
1 teaspoon vanilla
1 can (14 ounces) of pitted, tart, red cherries, drained (not pie filling)

Topping
1/2 cup graham cracker crumbs
3 egg whites
1/8 teaspoon cream of tartar

PROCEDURE

Crust
- Cream sugar and butter.
- Add 1 cup graham cracker crumbs and combine thoroughly.
- Pat in bottom of 9-inch springform pan. (I lightly butter the bottom of the pan before putting in the crumb mixture to ease removing the slices later.)

Custard
- In a double boiler, combine all ingredients and cook over medium-high heat, stirring constantly, until mixture is thick and creamy and has a pudding-like consistency. This part is important, otherwise custard may be too runny or too firm. We want a firm but creamy texture. This cooking should take about 15 to 20 minutes.
- Add cherries to custard mixture and allow to cool for 15 to 20 minutes.
- Pour mixture over graham cracker crust in springform pan.

Topping
- Sprinkle 1/2 cup graham cracker crumbs over top of custard.
- Beat the 3 egg whites with the cream of tartar until stiff but not dry.
- Spread mixture on top and bake at 350 degrees until meringue is golden.
- Cool and refrigerate until ready to serve.

NOTES

My mother made this dessert when it was her turn to hostess the afternoon bridge club (usually two tables of four). After the card playing, luncheon cloths were placed on the card tables and dessert and coffee were served. Everyone was gone by 4 p.m., in time to start the evening meal for the family.

NO-BAKE CHERRY TORTE

INGREDIENTS

1 package (12 ounces) of vanilla sugar wafer cookies (the kind with a layer of filling),
    ground fine (about 4 cups)

1/2 cup (1 stick) butter, softened

1 cup powdered sugar

2 eggs, separated

3/4 quart cherries

1 teaspoon vanilla

1 cup whipping cream

PROCEDURE

- Pat 3/4 (about 3 cups) of the ground vanilla wafers in bottom of a 10 x 7 pan.
- Cream butter and sugar and add slightly beaten egg yolks and mix thoroughly.
- Beat egg whites until stiff.
- Fold butter mixture into beaten egg whites.
- Spread mixture over the wafer crust, add cherries, and spread whipped cream on top.
- Sprinkle remaining wafer crumbs (1 cup) on top of the whipped cream.
- Refrigerate.

NOTES

This is my mother-in-law's recipe, but my wife prefers it made with raspberries. If fresh raspberries can't be found, a 24-ounce container of frozen raspberries will work almost as well.

CHOCOLATE CHERRY CREME PIE

INGREDIENTS

18 chocolate sandwich cookies (such as Oreos)

2 tablespoons butter, melted

1 small box vanilla pudding and pie filling mix (don't use instant)

2 cups red pitted cherries, including juice (frozen or canned, if fresh is not available)

1 cup milk

1 pint whipping cream

PROCEDURE

- Crush 12 of the cookies and mix with melted butter.
- Spread mixture on bottom of 9-inch pie plate to form crust.
- Separate other 6 cookies and stand the halves around the edge of the pie plate.
- In medium-size saucepan, stir together pudding mix, cherries, and milk.
- Cook over medium heat until thick, stirring constantly (about 5 minutes).
- Cool.
- Whip cream, reserving 3/4 cup for the top.
- Fold remainder of whipped cream into the cooled cherry mixture.
- Pour into pie crust.
- Refrigerate several hours.
- To serve, spread reserved whipped cream on top and garnish with shaved chocolate, if desired.

NOTES

This recipe won first place in a recipe contest sponsored by the Wisconsin Red Cherry Growers Association and the Wisconsin Department of Agriculture.

CHERRY CRUNCH

INGREDIENTS

2 cans (each 21 ounces) cherry pie filling

1 can (20 ounces) crushed pineapple, drained

1/3 cup nut pieces (walnuts or pecans)

1/2 cup (1 stick) butter, softened

1 package (18 and 1/2 ounces) yellow cake mix

PROCEDURE

- Butter or spray a 9 x 13 cake pan.
- Combine cherry pie filling, pineapple, and nuts.
- Spread on bottom of pan.
- Blend butter with cake mix—it will have a crumbly texture.
- Cover fruit/nut mixture.
- Bake at 350 degrees for 1 hour or until browned.

CHERRY DREAM BARS

INGREDIENTS

1 package (18 and 1/2 ounces) white cake mix

1/2 cup (1 stick) butter, softened and divided into 6 and 2 tablespoons portions

1 and 1/4 cups rolled oats, divided into 1 cup and 1/4 cup portions

1 egg

1 can (21 ounces) cherry pie filling

1/2 cup chopped nuts (your choice)

1/4 cup brown sugar, firmly packed

Whipped cream (optional)

PROCEDURE

- Grease or spray a 9 x 13 pan.
- In large bowl, combine cake mix, 6 tablespoons butter, and 1 cup oats.
- Mix until crumbly; set aside 1 cup of this mixture.
- To remaining crumb mixture, add egg and blend thoroughly.
- Press into prepared pan.
- Pour pie filling over crust, spreading evenly.
- To reserved crumbs, add remaining oats, butter, nuts, and sugar; mix thoroughly.
- Sprinkle over pie.
- Bake at 350 degrees for 30 to 40 minutes.
- Cool and serve with whipped cream, if desired.

NOTES

Makes about 12 servings. This is a favorite dessert at a restaurant in Saukville.

DRIED CHERRY OAT BRAN MUFFINS

INGREDIENTS

3/4 cup oat bran

1 and 1/2 cups flour

2 teaspoons baking powder

1/4 teaspoon salt

3/4 cup skim milk

1/4 cup honey

1 egg OR 2 egg whites

1/4 cup vegetable oil

1 cup (4 ounces) dried cherries

1/2 cup chopped nuts (your choice)

PROCEDURE

- Combine oat bran, flour, baking powder, and salt.
- Whisk together milk, honey, egg, and oil.
- Stir in dried cherries and nuts.
- Mix batter with dry ingredients.
- Bake at 375 degrees for 15 to 20 minutes.

NOTES

Makes 1 dozen muffins.

MULLED CHERRY GROG

INGREDIENTS

1 and 1/2 quarts apple cider or juice
1 and 1/2 quarts cherry juice
1 to 1 and 1/2 cups maple syrup
2 sticks cinnamon
6 whole cloves
Lemon slices for garnish

PROCEDURE

- Combine apple cider/juice, cherry juice, syrup, cinnamon, and cloves and heat thoroughly but do not boil.
- Remove cloves and serve with lemon slices.

NOTES

The word *grog* supposedly came from the nickname of British Admiral Edward Vernon (1684-1757). Old Grog tried to prevent scurvy in his crew by giving them a rum and water drink, which did nothing but warm their souls. The U.S. Navy gave sailors a ration of half a pint of distilled spirits per day served from a "grog tub." On land, grog became a popular stimulant among iron mill workers in the Northeast. Sweetened with molasses, it became known as blackstripe. A variation was called blackstrap. This cherry grog recipe is far less threatening!

CHERRIES JUBILEE

INGREDIENTS

3/4 cup cherry juice

3/4 cup water

1/3 cup sugar

1 and 1/2 tablespoons cornstarch

2 cups fresh, frozen, or canned red tart cherries

1/3 cup brandy (original recipe said this was optional, but I disagree)

Vanilla ice cream

PROCEDURE

- In medium saucepan combine cherry juice, water, and sugar.
- Over medium-high heat, bring to a boil.
- Add cornstarch to juice and mix until smooth.
- Cook slowly, stirring constantly until thickened and clear.
- Add cherries and cook about 2 minutes more or until thickened.
- Pour into heat-proof bowl or chafing dish.
- Heat brandy in small saucepan, ignite, and pour over cherry mixture.
- Blend and serve immediately over ice cream.

NOTES

Serves 6. This can provide a dramatic presentation for your dinner guests but, of course, be careful.

FISH BOIL

The subject of fish is covered more thoroughly in chapter 5, which deals with the North Woods region. The famous Door County fish boil, however, is in a category all by itself and is certainly worth special mention here. It's probably more showmanship than haute cuisine, but the end product is certainly tasty and proves also to be good food.

Here's how the show biz works: A huge kettle of salted water is boiling over a big fire. The cook lowers metal baskets in sequence, each with a separate ingredient (potatoes, onions, Lake Michigan whitefish or trout, maybe carrots) so that each is cooked properly and all will be ready at the same time. The spectators are already standing far back from the fire because of the heat, but when the cook throws kerosene (never gasoline) onto the fire there is an awesome fiery spiral that keeps them at a distance. At about the same time, the water in the kettle boils over carrying off all the fats, as well as dousing down the flames and fire. And supper is served!

Restaurants throughout Wisconsin are having outdoor fish boils now, and often they vary the menu with salmon, cod, or lobster in place of whitefish or trout.

If you don't have a thirty-gallon kettle or dozens of people to feed, you can do an indoor fish boil right on top of your stove. No hot flames or kerosene smell and certainly not as dramatic—just a supper reminiscent of summertime in beautiful Door County.

INDOOR FISH BOIL

INGREDIENTS

2 and 1/2 quarts water (about 10 cups)

1/3 cup salt

12 or so red potatoes

6 onions, cut up

Head of cabbage, cut into 6 or 8 wedges

2 pounds boned fish fillets (preferably whitefish)

PROCEDURE

- In large kettle, bring water and salt to a boil.
- Add potatoes and onions and simmer until done (about 20 to 30 minutes).
- Add cabbage and simmer another 10 minutes or more if needed.
- Add the fish and simmer 3 to 5 minutes more.
- With slotted spoon, serve portions to serving plates.

NOTES

Provide lemon wedges. This may be served with horseradish sauce or melted butter and sprinkled with chopped parsley. A little coleslaw and buttered rye bread top off this meal.

CENTRAL WISCONSIN RIVER COUNTRY

CHAPTER FOUR

ADAMS

COLUMBIA

JUNEAU

MARATHON

MARQUETTE

PORTAGE

SAUK

WOOD

This area is the smallest of the six defined regions, but its food has influenced not only Wisconsin but the rest of the world.

Baraboo in Sauk County was the winter home for the Ringling Brothers Circus. Five different circuses merged in 1882, including the Ringling Brothers Classic and Comic Company and became known as the Greatest Show on Earth. Today, circus memorabilia and restored original circus wagons are on display at the Circus World Museum in Baraboo. But equally deserving of the adjective "greatest" are the two original Wisconsin cheeses developed in this area, as well as two crops, ginseng and cranberries.

Marathon County grows 95 percent of the cultivated ginseng in the United States. Ginseng is the aromatic root of a plant native to China and North America where it grows wild. But before you go looking for it, be aware that it cannot be harvested without a license. Commercially, it is a very difficult crop to grow and requires a large investment. Pea-size seeds are placed in cool, moist, sandy soil where they stay for one year. It takes six months for seedlings to appear and four to seven years of cultivation before any actual harvest begins. In winter the ginseng plants are covered with straw to protect them from frost; in summer, they are sprayed to prevent diseases and covered with a slatted contrivance. In late autumn the slatted sections are slanted so snow won't break the lathes. After harvest in mid-October, the soil is generally barren. Replacing the depleted nutrients so that other crops can be grown is another lengthy process.

The cranberry is another native plant (its European cousin is the lingonberry). Cranberries grew wild in the acid bogs of central Wisconsin, and while early Wisconsin Indians picked and traded them, the real harvesting didn't begin until 1860 when settlers recognized that they were edible and could survive in soil that was of little use for anything else. My Aunt Emma worked "on the marsh" during harvest time, sorting the good cranberries from the bad. A test of quality was called the cranberry bounce (good name for a new dance?) whereby the berries were given seven chances to bounce over a wooden baffle onto the sorting belt. If they failed, they were vanquished to the slush pile. I wonder if cranberry juice was made from the failed berry pile?

If you play the word association game and mention Wisconsin, the immediate response is "cheese." Wisconsin was originally a wheat-producing state, but with soil depletion and competition from other states dairying gradually took over, despite some resistance. And now Wisconsin is the Dairy State! The importance of dairying prompted the University of Wisconsin to set up the College of Agriculture in the late 1800s and the first Dairymen's Association to be founded in Fond du Lac on January 15, 1870. Feeling so passionate about the dairy industry, the state legislature actually passed a law in 1935 requiring restaurants to serve Wisconsin butter and cheese with each meal. To discourage people from switching from butter to margarine, in 1932 the Wisconsin legislature taxed oleo (as oleomargarine was then called) and in 1935 forbade oleo to be colored. Wisconsin stores sold an unappetizing, lard-like margarine that came in a plastic bag. In the bag was a small pellet of yellow food coloring to squeeze and knead throughout the contents until it acquired the look of butter. Many Wisconsin residents drove to Illinois to buy colored margarine.

It's impossible to do justice to Wisconsin's 250 varieties and more than two billion pounds of cheese. As you might guess from those statistics, Wisconsin makes more cheese than any other state—one third of the nation's total. It's enough simply to say that most consumers consider the quality of Wisconsin cheese to be the best. And the demand continues to grow despite cholesterol awareness. One reason is that up-scale dining has created a demand for specialty cheeses; another is that the "grazing" style of eating often includes cheese. String cheese is a good example of a new, fun-to-eat light snack.

If we continue to play the word association game, "Wisconsin" doesn't necessarily suggest "potatoes." Agreed, Idaho has that honor, but Wisconsin can still hold its potato-head self-confidently high. Its production of round red, russet, and round white potatoes earns Wisconsin fifth place in potato growing.

A little potato trivia: Peruvians used potatoes (which the Quechua Indians called *papa*) as a decoration; ladies in the French court wore potato blossoms in their hair; and Louis XVI wore them in his lapel to encourage the growing of potatoes. The word *spud* is a misuse of Gaelic and Cockney English words used to describe a type of spade used to dig potatoes.

The use of the word *tuber* to refer to potatoes probably comes from a shortened version of the Latin name for potatoes, *Solamun tuberosum*. The Spanish word for potato is *patata*, from the Haitian word *batata*. The Spanish took the potato to Europe from South America—hence, the Haitian connection.

So this Central Wisconsin River Country region has contributed to the world's bread basket by growing the lowly and ever popular potato, cleverly using otherwise unusable land to grow cranberries, beating out some Asian countries by growing a better ginseng, and finally by creating and producing three world-class cheeses (with due deference to Switzerland, France, and all the other cheese nations).

GINSENG

A sixteenth-century Jesuit missionary in China, familiar with the Chinese use of ginseng in herbal medicines, theorized that it might also grow in Canada. Somehow, a Canadian Jesuit in 1716 read about the thesis, began looking for wild ginseng, and found it. Within a few years French fur traders and Indian helpers were gathering it for shipment to China. Even the American pioneer Daniel Boone supplemented his income by gathering wild ginseng.

Wisconsin has been cultivating the ginseng root since 1890 and currently has more than 1,300 growers of this uncommon crop—1,100 of them in Marathon County. Their efforts represent 90 percent of all U.S.-grown ginseng and Wisconsin's second largest cash crop after cranberries.

Of the total crop of two million pounds of dry ginseng roots, 98 percent is exported, primarily to Hong Kong, where its higher quality brings as much as six times more than Chinese or Korean ginseng. In the late 1880s it was selling at sixty dollars a pound, but currently the price is only five to ten dollars per pound (about the same as a good pound of chocolate!) due in part to large-scale cultivation of ginseng in Ontario and British Columbia, Canada. It doesn't take an economist to realize that this represents the competition of the global marketplace—great for the consumer but not so great for the grower.

The word *ginseng* comes from the Chinese *jen shen* ("image of man"), since the root resembles the human torso and limbs. Ginseng is considered to be a source of vitality and strength and a stress reliever. It is used as food (it has a licorice taste and is an excellent soup base) but more often as medicine. In addition to a host of maladies (nausea, dizziness, amnesia, asthma) it is said to cure, ginseng is rumored to be an aphrodisiac. Its use is not government regulated, however, because the U.S. Food and Drug Administration categorizes ginseng as an herb and not a drug. Early Wisconsin Potawatomi Indians discovered the medicinal uses for the root and pounded it into a poultice to cure earaches or liquefied it to produce an eyewash. The largest grower in Wisconsin, Hsu's Ginseng Enterprises of Wausau, considers its products to be the "Root to Health." Hsu's supplied me with the three ginseng recipes that follow.

SEX MUFFINS

INGREDIENTS

1 and 3/4 cups all-purpose flour

2 teaspoons baking powder

1 teaspoon ginger

1 teaspoon cinnamon

1 tablespoon ginseng powder (contents of 15 500-mg. capsules; see notes below)

2 ounces semisweet chocolate

6 ounces miniature chocolate chips

1/2 stick (4 tablespoons) butter

1/3 cup honey

1 cup milk

2 egg whites, slightly beaten

Raisins (optional)

PROCEDURE

- In medium to large bowl, mix together flour, baking powder, spices, and ginseng powder.
- In double boiler, slowly melt semisweet chocolate, chocolate chips, and butter until smooth.
- Add melted ingredients to dry mixture.
- Add honey, milk, and egg whites and stir just enough to blend.
- Pour mixture into greased muffin tins.
- Bake in at 400 degrees for 20 to 25 minutes or until brown.
- Allow muffins to cool two minutes before removing from pan.

NOTES

The reputation of ginseng as an aphrodisiac explains the name of these muffins (just don't eat too many). If you cannot find the ginseng capsules at your local pharmacy or health food store, they can be ordered directly from Hsu's Ginseng Enterprises in Wausau, (800) 388-3818.

GINSENG & BEEF

INGREDIENTS

1/2 pound of tenderloin, cut into narrow strips or chunks

Soy sauce

Sherry wine

Sugar

Fresh ginseng root, thoroughly cleaned

Black pepper

Garlic powder

Vegetable oil

3 or 4 small green onions

PROCEDURE

- Marinate the beef with a mixture of soy sauce, sherry wine, and sugar.
- Slice the ginseng root into thin slices.
- Stir-fry the meat in vegetable oil.
- Add the ginseng slices and continue frying briefly, while adding black pepper, garlic powder, and the soy/sherry/sugar sauce to taste.
- Add the green onions and cook briefly.

NOTES

If you cannot find ginseng roots locally, they can be ordered from Hsu's Ginseng in Wausau, (800) 388-3818.

TOSSED GINSENG SALAD

INGREDIENTS

1 small head of either lettuce or cabbage, coarsely shredded

1 fresh ginseng root, thoroughly cleaned and sliced

Several spinach leaves torn into small pieces

1 small onion (red or white), sliced into rings

1 or 2 green onion stalks, julienned 1 inch

Optional additional ingredients: soy sauce, sugar, sesame seeds, black pepper

PROCEDURE

- Combine all ingredients and toss well.
- Serve with oil and vinegar or your favorite dressing.

NOTES

This recipe will probably not win a salad contest prize, but I have included it to point out that ginseng can be used in many different ways. If you cannot find ginseng roots locally, they can be ordered from Hsu's Ginseng in Wausau, (800) 388-3818.

CRANBERRIES

Cranberries were in the Native American diet long before the Pilgrims landed. In addition to eating them for food, they also used them to concoct medicines and dyes. Their word for them was *sassamanesh*. The Pilgrims thought that the cranberry flower resembled the water-wading crane. Having never seen a cranberry flower, I have to accept their perception that the flower's pistil and closely arranged stamens projecting downward look like (with some imagination) the long-legged crane. Clever people that they were, they added the word *berry* to *crane*. *Cranberry* certainly is a lot easier to say than *sassamanesh*!

Wild cranberries were plentiful in the low-lying wetlands along the Massachusetts coast and, perhaps because of this head start, Massachusetts ranked number one in cranberry production for many years. But as settlers trekked west they discovered the wild cranberries also in the wetlands of central Wisconsin. Only five states have the unique wetland environment that cranberries need: Massachusetts, New Jersey, Oregon, Washington, and Wisconsin. As the cranberry gained in popularity and the acid bog lands weren't of much use in growing other crops, commercial cranberry production began about 1860. Edward Sacket, of New York State, gets credit for that development.

Wisconsin has thousands of acres in cranberry production, and eighteen Wisconsin counties produce nearly one third of all U.S. cranberries, making Wisconsin number one in yield since 1995. Although there are more than 100 different types of cranberries, only five varieties account for most of Wisconsin's—Searles, McFarlin, Homes, Stevens, and Ben Liar (some named after the men who cultivated them). The village of Warrens (Monroe County in the neighboring Hidden Valleys area) is known as the Cranberry Capital of Wisconsin.

Only 10 percent of all U.S. cranberries are used fresh; the other 90 percent become juice, jam, or "craisins" (dried cranberries).

For many years cranberries were generally served only at Thanksgiving or Christmas. But their recent discovery by talented chefs and scientific claims that cranberry juice purifies the blood (and offers a generous amount of vitamin C) have generated a new interest in using cranberries throughout the year. Since fresh cranberries are almost impossible to find when they're not in season (the season is September-October), it's a smart idea to buy several packages and pop them in the freezer. If you buy them bulk, wash, sort, and discard any soft ones. Let them dry and then freeze them in your own freezer containers or bags.

Cranberries provide both a tart and sweet flavor enrichment for other cooked fruits and vegetables. A handful of berries marries (aren't those words fun to say together?) well with apple pie in both taste and color. They're perfect cousins in pecan tarts or rolls, and a few handfuls added to glazed carrots radiate sunshine and healthfulness. Add some to any bread, muffin, or pancake batter or to a fruit compote for an excellent salad.

Because of the high acidity of cranberries, sauce will keep for ten to fourteen days in the refrigerator and for an entire season in the freezer.

The American Institute for Cancer Research has provided the following excellent suggestions for using cranberries to flavor low-fat dishes:

• Cook 4 ounces of cranberries in one cup of orange juice until they pop. Use as a low-fat sauce over green vegetables.

• Add 1/2 cup ground or chopped cranberries to corn meal or other low-fat stuffing for the holiday fowl.

• Before baking apples, fill the center with cranberries and sprinkle a little sugar and cinnamon on top.

• For a fantastic pie filling, combine chopped cranberries with chopped, fresh, or dried naturally sweet fruits such as raisins, prunes, apricots, or apples.

• Add 1/2 to 1 cup coarsely chopped cranberries to any bread or muffin recipe.

CRANBERRY COLESLAW

INGREDIENTS

1/4 cup sliced fresh cranberries

1 tablespoon honey

1 teaspoon celery salt

Salt, to taste

1/4 cup mayonnaise

1 teaspoon vinegar

3 cups cabbage, finely shredded

PROCEDURE

- Combine cranberries, honey, celery salt, and let stand 15 minutes.
- Add mayonnaise and vinegar.
- Mix well.
- Pour over cabbage, add additional salt if desired.
- Toss.

FROZEN CRANBERRY SALAD OR DESSERT

INGREDIENTS

3 cups (or a 12-ounce package) fresh cranberries, finely chopped or ground

1 and 1/2 cups sugar

1/2 cup nuts, chopped (walnuts or pecans)

1 can (8 and 1/4 ounces) crushed pineapple, drained

1 package (8 ounces) cream cheese, softened

1 cup (1/2 pint) whipping cream, whipped

PROCEDURE

- In medium to large bowl, combine cranberries and sugar.
- Add nuts and pineapple and mix well.
- Gradually add cream cheese and mix until well blended.
- Fold in whipped cream.
- Put in mold OR in cupcake papers (makes 12 full ones).
- Freeze.
- When ready to serve, remove from freezer and place in refrigerator for about 10 minutes to remove some of the hardness.

NOTES

I use this recipe time and time again and everyone always likes it. To serve as a salad, place portions on a bed of shredded lettuce (my guests seem to leave the lettuce leaf if I put one under this salad). To serve as a dessert, top it with a little shaved chocolate or a dab of whipped cream and a cookie on the side. If you use cupcake papers, be sure to remove them before serving. Individual portions work much better than a mold, which has to be sliced.

CRANBERRY NUT BREAD

INGREDIENTS

2 cups all-purpose flour

1 cup sugar

1 and 1/2 teaspoons baking powder

1 teaspoon salt

1/2 teaspoon baking soda

2 tablespoons shortening

1 tablespoon grated orange peel

3/4 cup orange juice

1 egg, well beaten

1 cup cranberries, fresh or frozen, coarsely chopped

1/2 cup chopped nuts (walnuts or pecans)

PROCEDURE

- In medium to large bowl, combine flour, sugar, baking powder, salt, and baking soda.
- Add shortening, orange peel, orange juice, and egg.
- Mix until well blended.
- Stir in cranberries and nuts.
- Grease bottom only of a 9 x 5 loaf pan.
- Pour batter into pan and bake at 350 degrees for 55 to 60 minutes until cake tester comes out clean.
- Cool thoroughly before serving.

NOTES

Makes one loaf. Check during the last 10 or 15 minutes of baking time and if edges appear to be getting crusty and the center is not thoroughly baked, place a piece of foil lightly over the top. The foil cover allows the center to get done and prevents the edges from being overdone.

CRANBERRY TURKEY TACOS

INGREDIENTS

1 can (8 ounces) jellied cranberry sauce

1/2 cup mild picante sauce

2 tablespoons Worcestershire sauce

1/2 teaspoon garlic powder

1/4 teaspoon ground cumin

2 cups cooked, shredded turkey

10 taco shells

For garnish: shredded lettuce, chopped tomatoes, chopped onion, shredded cheese

PROCEDURE

- In medium saucepan, combine all ingredients except taco shells and garnishes.
- Mix thoroughly.
- Cook over medium heat until thickened (about 20 minutes), stirring occasionally.
- Spoon into taco shells and add garnishes.

NOTES

This recipe was presented at the 1992 Wisconsin Cranberry Festival in Warrens.

CRANBERRY BEEF STEW

INGREDIENTS

3 tablespoons butter

1/2 cup chopped onion

2 cloves garlic, chopped

3 pounds lean beef, cut into 2-inch cubes

Seasoned flour (flour, salt, pepper, or seasoned salt)

2 cups beef bouillon (use a beef soup base mix)

1 cup red wine

1 cup tomatoes, peeled and chopped

4 cups fresh cranberries (can be left whole)

1 tablespoon sugar

1 bay leaf

1 teaspoon thyme

1 cup celery, chopped

1 cup green beans, cut in half

6 carrots, peeled and cut in pieces

Parsley for garnish, if desired

PROCEDURE

- In large Dutch oven or heavy kettle, melt butter and sauté chopped onion and garlic until soft.
- Roll beef cubes in the seasoned flour.
- Brown the beef in the kettle over high heat for 3 to 5 minutes.
- Add remaining ingredients, except celery, green beans, and carrots.
- Simmer mixture for 1 and 1/4 hours.
- Add the celery, green beans, and carrots and continue cooking, covered, for another 45 minutes or until meat and vegetables are tender.

NOTES

This will make 12 to 15 servings but leftovers always seem to be better the next day after the flavors have had more time to co-mingle. This recipe was a winner in the 1991 Wisconsin Cranberry Festival in Warrens.

CRANBERRY PORK CHOPS

INGREDIENTS

4 pork chops, 1 inch thick
2 tablespoons cooking oil
1/2 cup dry red wine
1/2 cup honey
1 cup fresh cranberries (can be left whole or cut in half)
Salt/pepper

PROCEDURE

- In skillet, brown pork chops in hot oil.
- Season with salt and pepper.
- Drain off any excess fat.
- Combine wine and honey and pour over chops.
- Cover and simmer 1 hour.
- During last 10 minutes, add cranberries.

NOTES

This is a favorite recipe of the Wisconsin Cranberry Growers. A little poem from an 1893 cranberry cookbook goes as follows:

> To be healthy, wealthy, wise;
> To save the life that we all prize,
> This one thing, I advise —
> Eat cranberries!

CRAISIN-GLAZED STEAK

INGREDIENTS

1/2 cup craisins (dried cranberries)

1/2 cup chopped onion

1 large garlic clove

2 tablespoons brown sugar

1/2 teaspoon dry mustard

1/2 teaspoon pepper

1 teaspoon liquid smoke (if you don't have it, skip it)

2 tablespoons vegetable oil

1/2 cup chili sauce

1/2 cup water

2 boneless top loin beef steaks, cut 1 inch thick (about 1 and 3/4 pounds)

PROCEDURE

- In a food processor, combine craisins, onion, garlic, brown sugar, dry mustard, and pepper.
- Process until finely chopped.
- Add liquid smoke, oil, chili sauce, and water.
- Process until well mixed.
- Transfer mixture to a small saucepan.
- Simmer for 10 to 12 minutes, stirring occasionally.
- Place steaks on broiler rack that has been sprayed with a nonstick oil.
- Season with salt/pepper to taste.
- Broil 4 inches from heat for 7 minutes.
- Turn steaks and spread tops and sides with glaze.
- Broil 7 more minutes or until desired doneness.
- To serve: Steaks may be cut in half or thinly sliced.

NOTES

Makes 4 servings. This recipe is from the 1990 "Best of the Cranberry Festival" recipe booklet, Warrens, Wisconsin.

CRANBERRY APPLE PIE

INGREDIENTS

Pastry for two 9-inch pie crusts

1 cup white sugar

1/2 cup brown sugar

1/3 cup all-purpose flour

1 teaspoon apple pie spice

1 quart tart apples, peeled and sliced

2 cups cranberries, fresh or frozen (whole or halved)

2 tablespoons butter

PROCEDURE

- In medium to large bowl, stir together sugars, flour, and spice.
- In pastry-lined pie pan, alternate layers of apples, cranberries, and sugar mixture, beginning and ending with apples.
- Dot with butter.
- Cover with top pie crust.
- Cut slits in crust, seal, and flute edges.
- Bake at 425 degrees for 40 to 50 minutes.
- Cool.

NOTES

As with any apple pie, a piece of cheese and a scoop of vanilla ice cream are always good additions.

CRANBERRY CAKE WITH CARAMEL SAUCE

INGREDIENTS

Cake

1 and 1/2 cups all-purpose flour

1 and 1/8 cups sugar

1 and 1/2 teaspoons baking powder

3/8 teaspoon salt

3 tablespoons butter, softened

3/4 cup milk

2 full cups cranberries, fresh or frozen, cut in half

Caramel Sauce

1/2 cup butter

1/2 cup white sugar

1/2 cup light brown sugar

1/2 cup whipping cream

PROCEDURE

Cake

- Combine flour, sugar, baking powder, and salt.
- Cut in butter with a pastry blender.
- Add milk, stir lightly, add cranberries, and stir well.
- Butter and flour an 8 x 8 or 9 x 9 baking dish.
- Bake at 375 degrees for 30 to 40 minutes.
- Cool.

Caramel Sauce

- Melt butter in double boiler.
- Add remaining ingredients.
- Cook 25 minutes.

To serve

- Cut cake into 9 square serving pieces.
- Put small amount of heated caramel sauce on bottom of plate.
- Place cake square on top of sauce.
- Douse top of cake square with more caramel sauce.

NOTES

This family recipe comes from a guest chef on my TV food series (*The Foods That Made Wisconsin Famous*). This really is an outstandingly delicious cake and sauce. The sauce can also be used on ice cream.

CRANBERRIES JUBILEE

INGREDIENTS

1 cup sugar

1 and 1/2 cups water

2 cups (1/2 pound) fresh cranberries, whole or cut in half

1/4 cup brandy

PROCEDURE

- In medium saucepan, combine sugar and water, stirring to dissolve sugar.
- Bring to a boil and boil for 5 minutes.
- Add cranberries, return to a boil, and cook another 5 minutes.
- Turn into heat-proof bowl or chafing dish.
- In small pan, heat brandy, ignite, and pour over cranberry mixture.
- Blend into sauce and serve immediately over ice cream.

NOTES

This is, of course, similar to Cherries Jubilee, but I did want to show that it isn't always just cherries that have the opportunity to be jubilant.

POTATOES

One potato, two potato, three potato, four—this children's nursery rhyme was never meant to go up to 2.7 billion! But that's how many pounds Wisconsin's 300 potato farmers grew in 1997 on their 84,000 acres. Wisconsin is the third largest potato grower after Idaho and Washington, but it is the only state to grow all four major potato varieties: (1) russet (Burbank, Norkorah, Centennials, Frontiers), the best-selling, brown-skinned, oblong potato that is the classic baking potato as well as the best choice for french fries; (2) round whites (Superior—the potato chip potato—Katahdin, Kennebec, White Rose), best for boiling, mashing or using in potato salads; (3) round red (Red Pontiac, Norland, Red LaSoda, Larouge, Sangre, McClure), a moist potato good for American fries, hash browns, potato salad, scalloped potatoes, or potato pancakes; (4) yellow flesh or finish, a relatively new category often known as Yukon Gold. Though a little on the expensive side, they are absolutely delicious. From their natural color and taste, you'd think lots of butter has been added.

Potatoes were once regarded as a food for cattle and the poor, but now they are a staple for everyone. And the nice thing about potatoes is that there is nothing bad to say about them. They have no fat or cholesterol and are low in sodium. One potato provides half of one's daily need for vitamin C, along with vitamin B-6, thiamin, niacin, iron, magnesium, potassium (more than bananas), and lots of dietary fiber. A five-ounce potato has only 110 calories. So why are potatoes considered fattening? Solely because we abuse this nutritional powerhouse by covering it with gravy, butter, or sour cream. It's our own fault!

When baking potatoes, do not wrap them in foil. It's convenient for restaurants to cook them that way, but the foil traps the steam given off in baking and produces a soggy potato. After a potato is baked, however, it can be wrapped in foil and kept warm for at least the next 45 minutes.

Store potatoes in a cool, dark area in a well-ventilated container (I use a basket). Too much light causes the potatoes to turn green, but if they do just cut away the green part.

I hope you're convinced that Wisconsin potatoes are the perfect food item for any and all occasions. You can serve them plain and simple or in grand style with panache!

POTATO-BROCCOLI-CHEESE SOUP

INGREDIENTS

3 cups chicken broth (chicken soup base will work)

1 cup chopped onion

2 cups diced potatoes

1 cup cut broccoli

4 tablespoons butter

4 tablespoons flour

1 teaspoon salt

2 cups milk

8 ounces shredded Swiss cheese

Dash white pepper

Dash dill weed (optional)

PROCEDURE

- In large saucepan, combine chicken broth, onion, potatoes, and broccoli.
- Bring mixture to boiling.
- Reduce heat, cover, and simmer until vegetables are tender.
- Remove half the vegetables, place in blender; and blend until smooth (about 1/2 to 1 minute).
- Pour blended vegetables back into unblended vegetables in saucepan.
- In another saucepan, melt butter.
- Blend in flour and salt.
- Add milk all at once.
- Cook and stir until mixture is thickened and bubbly.
- Stir in shredded cheese until melted.
- Pour mixture into vegetable saucepan and heat thoroughly.
- Add pepper to taste and dill weed.

NOTES

Serves 6 to 8. This recipe won second prize in a 1988 contest sponsored by the Wisconsin Department of Agriculture.

MASHED POTATO BREAD STICKS

INGREDIENTS

1 medium potato, cooked, peeled, and mashed (reserve 2/3 cup of the potato water)

3 and 1/2 cups all-purpose flour, divided into 1 and 1/2-, and 2-cup portions

1 package (1/4 ounce) active dry yeast OR 2 and 1/4 teaspoons of the rapid-rise yeast that comes in the 4-ounce jars

1/4 cup vegetable oil

1 teaspoon sugar

1 teaspoon salt

1 egg white

1 tablespoon water

Sesame seeds

PROCEDURE

- Grease 2 baking sheets and set aside.
- Heat the reserved potato water in small pan to 120 to 130 degrees (here's where that cooking thermometer comes in handy).
- In large bowl, combine potato, warm potato water, 1 and 1/2 cups flour, yeast, oil, sugar, and salt.
- Beat with electric mixer on high for 2 minutes.
- Stir in remaining flour.
- Divide dough into 20 to 24 equal parts.
- Roll each part into 1/2- to 3/4-inch ropes and place, about 1 inch apart, on the greased cookie sheets.
- Cover with oiled wax paper and let rest 20 minutes.
- Remove wax paper.
- In small bowl, whisk egg white and I tablespoon water.
- Brush over bread sticks.
- Sprinkle sticks with sesame seeds.
- Bake at 350 degrees for 25 to 30 minutes or until golden brown. (I bake them until they are a deep gold because I like the sticks more crunchy than soft.)

NOTES

The first time I saw this recipe I thought it was dumb, but these potato bread sticks are quite good and it's fun to say to a guest, "Have one of these mashed potato bread sticks." Chances are, they never had one before.

POTATO APPLE SALAD

INGREDIENTS

4 to 5 medium red potatoes

4 to 5 medium white potatoes

2 hard-cooked eggs, sliced

1 medium McIntosh or Empire apple (an Empire apple is a cross between a McIntosh and a Red Delicious), diced

1 stalk celery, diced

1 medium dill pickle, diced

1/2 cup mayonnaise

1/2 cup Miracle Whip

2 tablespoons apple cider vinegar

1/4 cup canola oil

Salt/pepper to taste

PROCEDURE

- Boil potatoes in skins, peel, and slice.
- Combine all ingredients.

NOTES

This is another family recipe handed down from a good friend. The combination of apples and potatoes is unusual, and it's all the other ingredients combined that give this salad such a unique flavor. Generally, I have avoided mentioning brand names, but here I must say that it's important to use Miracle Whip in addition to regular mayonnaise. If you use all of one or all of the other, you'll lose an essential flavor combination.

GERMAN POTATO SALAD

INGREDIENTS

6 medium red salad potatoes, cooked, peeled, and sliced

3 to 4 slices bacon, diced

1 diced onion

1 tablespoon cornstarch

1/2 cup sugar

1/2 cup vinegar

1/2 cup water

Salt/pepper to taste

Hard-cooked eggs (optional)

PROCEDURE

- Cook potatoes with peels on; do not overcook; when they come to a boil, it should be just about right. Potatoes should be cooked throughout but still firm—test by poking a fork into them
- Cool potatoes for 10 minutes, then peel and slice.
- Fry bacon until crisp, remove, and drain on paper toweling.
- In bacon grease, sauté onions until tender.
- Remove from heat, put bacon crisp back in skillet with onions, and set aside.
- In small bowl, combine cornstarch and sugar.
- In another small bowl, combine vinegar and water (an inexpensive vinegar is better than a more costly brand, which is often too strong for this recipe).
- Combine dry and wet ingredients and add to bacon/onion skillet.
- Stir constantly until mixture becomes thick and appears glossy (this is a critical step).
- Pour over potatoes and let sit for about 1/2 hour—do not stir at this point.
- After the half hour, stir gently to coat the potato slices, being careful not to break them.
- Serve warm or at room temperature.
- If salad is to be served later, refrigerate it and then allow it to warm to room temperature.
- Sliced hard-cooked eggs make an excellent garnish

NOTES

There may be lots of German potato salad recipes but this is my mother's, which she learned from her mother, and without a doubt it is the best (or am I slightly prejudiced?).

GOLDEN OVEN-ROASTED POTATOES & CHEESE

INGREDIENTS

3 pounds red potatoes

1/2 pound sharp cheddar cheese (use only a sharp cheddar), in 1/2-inch cubes

1/2 to 1 stick butter

Salt to taste

White pepper (a bit more tangy than black pepper and leaves no black specks)

PROCEDURE

- Lightly butter a 13 x 9 cake pan or similar size baking dish.
- Parboil potatoes until not quite done and still firm.
- Cool, peel, and dice into 1/2-inch cubes.
- Layer potatoes on bottom of pan or baking dish.
- Season to taste.
- Distribute cheese cubes but don't cover potatoes completely.
- Add dots of butter.
- Repeat layers of potatoes, cheese, butter, and seasonings until used up.
- Bake at 300 degrees for 2 to 3 hours until top is crusty and golden brown.
- Every half hour or so, carefully fold over the potato layers with spatula—this is essential to get all the ingredients co-mingled and to prevent the top layer from getting overly crusty.

NOTES

This recipe can easily be scaled up or down, adding more or less cheese, as desired. This is my wife's recipe and when we invite guests and say that one of the dishes will be Carol's Potatoes and Cheese, they always respond enthusiastically.

MASHED POTATO BALLS

INGREDIENTS

A bowl of mashed potatoes (approximately 1/2 to 3/4 cup per ball)
Butter, melted
Salt to taste
White pepper to taste
1 egg, slightly beaten
Crushed corn flakes

PROCEDURE

- Combine potatoes, melted butter, salt, and pepper.
- Chill.
- Form into balls (somewhere between golf ball and tennis ball size).
- Roll in beaten egg and then in crushed corn flakes.
- Place balls on ungreased baking sheet and heat at 350 degrees for about 1/2 hour (any longer and they have a tendency to flatten out).

NOTES

You can use instant potatoes if you wish, but the balls will have a little less body. Garnish each potato ball with a sprig of parsley. Place the balls around beef/pork/ham slices or around a platter of turkey pieces. This recipe doesn't sound like anything special but it has a lot of merit:
- Can be made up a day in advance and held in refrigerator
- The balls don't take long to warm up
- Each family member or guest takes one or two balls—a unique way to serve ordinary mashed potatoes.

SCALLOPED POTATOES IN WINE

INGREDIENTS

4 to 6 potatoes, sliced thick

2 large onions, sliced thick

1 package (6 triangles) or 1/3 pound Gruyere cheese, crumbled

1 stick butter cut into small pieces

Salt

White pepper

White wine (sauterne works well)

PROCEDURE

- Place potatoes, onions, cheese, butter, and seasonings in layers in a deep pot (a bean pot works great).
- Pour in wine until it begins to bubble up.
- Cover tightly.
- Bake at 300 degrees for a minimum of 4 hours (it actually can go even longer, but with the great aroma you won't have the patience to wait much longer).

NOTES

This recipe came from a good friend, and my wife and I have made it countless times. It is simply superb and while the ingredients and procedures are simple, it makes a very profound "gourmet-cooking" statement.

THREE-CHEESE MASHED POTATOES

INGREDIENTS

3 pounds potatoes, cooked and mashed (slightly salted)

1 cup green pepper, diced

1 bunch sliced scallions

1/4 pound (1 stick) butter

1 small can minced pimentos with juice

6 ounces cream cheese

1/2 cup grated cheddar cheese

1/2 cup grated Parmesan cheese

PROCEDURE

- Sauté green pepper and scallions in butter.
- Add to potatoes.
- Gradually add remaining ingredients, beating constantly.
- Mixture should be fairly moist.
- Add additional cream and butter, if necessary, to achieve desired consistency.
- Put into ovenproof dish.
- Bake at 350 degrees, uncovered, for 30 minutes.

NOTES

This won first place in the 1988 recipe contest sponsored by the Wisconsin Potato Growers Auxiliary, Potato Industry Board, Potato and Vegetable Growers Association and the Wisconsin Department of Agriculture—an awesome list suggesting a competition harder to win than a Pillsbury Bake-Off!

POTATO CHIP COOKIES

INGREDIENTS

3 cups all-purpose flour

1 cup sugar

1 cup crushed potato chips

2 egg yolks

3/4 cup vegetable shortening

1/2 cup (1 stick) butter, softened

1 teaspoon vanilla

Powdered sugar

PROCEDURE

- In large bowl, combine all ingredients except powdered sugar.
- Beat with electric mixer until consistency of fine crumbs.
- Shape dough into 1- to 1 and 1/2-inch balls.
- Place on ungreased cookie sheets.
- Flatten balls with spatula.
- Bake at 350 degrees for 10 to 12 minutes or until lightly browned.
- Remove from baking sheet and dust with powdered sugar.

NOTES

Makes about 3 dozen. The recipe is from the Wisconsin Potato Growers Association cookbook, *The All-American Potato Cookbook*.

SPUDNUT KISSES

INGREDIENTS

2 and 1/2 cups flaked coconut (10- or 12-ounce package)

1 and 3/4 cups powdered sugar

1/3 cup mashed potatoes, chilled (when mashing, don't add any salt/pepper, butter, or milk)

1/2 teaspoon vanilla

4 squares (1 ounce each) semisweet chocolate, melted

PROCEDURE

- Combine all ingredients except chocolate.
- Form into bite-size balls and with a toothpick dip them into a combination of the chocolate and about 1/3 bar of melted paraffin (available in canning section of grocery store).
- The combination of chocolate and paraffin gives a professional coating and hardens like commercial candy bars.
- Place dipped balls or kisses on wax paper.
- Let coating harden at room temperature (this happens almost immediately), remove toothpicks, and store in airtight container. Sometimes I cover the hole the toothpick made with a little candy star (in small bottles in baking section of the grocery store).
- I spread any leftover chocolate on graham crackers for a little extra treat.

POTATO CANDY

INGREDIENTS

1 teaspoon vanilla

1/4 teaspoon salt

1/4 cup mashed potatoes, unseasoned

4 cups powdered sugar

1 cup creamy peanut butter

PROCEDURE

- Add vanilla and salt to mashed potatoes.
- Chill.
- Add powdered sugar to mixture slowly until stiff and dry.
- Divide into 3 parts.
- Roll one part to about 1/4-inch thickness on wax paper to form a rectangle about 4 by 12 inches.
- Spread with a thin layer of peanut butter.
- Roll up as for jelly roll.
- Repeat with remaining 2 parts potato mixture.
- Chill several hours.
- To serve, slice thin.
- Store in refrigerator

NOTES

Makes about 72 pieces. This is a regional (Arkansas) candy treat—they made do with what they had.

CHEESE

Cheese making was a practical way for farmers to use up surplus milk, since cheese would keep for long periods of time—an important consideration in the days before refrigeration. Before 1850 the task fell to the farmers' wives, somewhat to their distaste. It involved making rennet, which required killing a calf and removing its fourth stomach. An extract of the rennet membrane was the ingredient needed to curdle milk in the cheese-making process.

Writers disagree on who started the first actual cheese factory in Wisconsin and when. Some say it was Anne Pickett in 1841 on the family farm near Lake Mills. Others say it was Chester Hazen in 1864 near Fond du Lac, although Hiram Smith of Sheboygan County had a business card indicating his factory was established in 1860. Some even say Charles Rockwell had the first commercial cheese operation in the town of Koshkonong (Jefferson County) in 1837. The differences depend on the interpretation of cheese factories as independent of other farm operations or as separate entities developed exclusively for making cheese. The original cheese factories were cooperative ventures where milk was collected from many farmers, weighed, and credited to their accounts. Then when the cheese was made it was divided and apportioned among them. Often the cheese factory was nothing more than a log house. Today's all stainless-steel cheese factory has come a long way.

Less than 10 percent of the 2,807 cheese factories that were operating in 1922—the all-time high—are still producing. Today about 225 skilled, licensed, and knowledgeable cheese makers (more than in any other state) produce more than two billion pounds of cheese per year, about 30 percent of the nation's total.

Wisconsin ranks first in the production of American, Muenster, brick, limburger, Italian, and blue cheese; third in Swiss cheese; and fifth in cottage cheese curd. Most of it ends up on pizza, followed by sandwiches, salads, and appetizers.

Only three cheeses originated in America: liederkranz, brick, and Colby. The latter two are Wisconsin creations, and unfortunately liederkranz (from the German for "wreath of song") is no longer made. I'm told that the culture needed to make it has been lost. Its clientele was limited since it was pungent—one definitely had to acquire a taste for liederkranz—but it was called a "deodorized limburger,"

meaning, of course, that limburger is even more pungent. One writer described limburger as "a premeditated outrage upon the organs of smell." Limburger originated in Luttich, Belgium, and is made from skimmed milk allowed to partially decompose before pressing it into cheese. Many years ago a limburger rebellion took place in the town of Monroe (Green County). When about six wagonloads of limburger were left to "ripen" in the sun in front of the town bank, townspeople threatened an action similar to the Boston Tea Party. Finally, the cheese was removed and stored underground, out of sight and out of smell! I happen to like limburger occasionally and find it best eaten on crackers with raw, diced onions—what a snack!

Every grilled cheese sandwich lover is familiar with Colby cheese. It's mild, smooth, moist, and melts evenly. Joseph Steinwand introduced it at his father's factory near the small town of Colby, Marathon County in the late 1800s.

Colby a form of cheddar in which the curd is cooled in cold water and then pressed into forms and aged. The drier cheddar is molded immediately and then repeatedly rotated to extrude all the excess whey. Some say Mr. Steinwand's batch of cheddar cheese was "going well"; others say he left the factory and when he returned the next day the batch had taken a turn from "well" to "bad." Still others (probably close friends) say that he knew what he was doing and in fact was experimenting to produce a new and different cheese. A few detractors say that Mr. Steinwand actually learned the process of making Colby from another cheese maker, Lawrence Wertz. So who really knows? Mr. Steinwand originally called the cheese Steinwand Colby in honor of himself and the town of Colby. We know it now as just Colby, and it remains one of the most popular cheeses.

Wisconsin's other original cheese is brick cheese, from the 1870s. Full credit for its creation goes to Swiss immigrant John Jossie. Brick cheese is very smooth, has small holes, and is produced by putting the curd into brick-shaped forms and pressing out the whey. The "bricks" are rubbed with salt for three days and then allowed to ripen slowly for two to three months.

Some people liken brick cheese to Emmentaler, or Swiss cheese. Some call it the "married man's limburger," since its distinct aroma is politely inoffensive yet reminiscent of limburger's "bouquet."

CHEESE-COVERED GRAPE HORS D'OEUVRES

INGREDIENTS

8 ounces Wisconsin blue cheese, softened

10 ounces cream cheese, softened

Green seedless grapes, washed and dried (about 60)

Crushed nuts (pecans recommended)

Pretzel sticks

PROCEDURE

- Blend the two cheeses and chill.
- Form about 1 teaspoon of the cheese mixture around each grape.
- Roll in crushed nuts.
- Refrigerate.
- To serve, insert pretzel stick into each ball (grasp pretzel stick at the end so it won't break) but not too long before serving or they'll soften and break off—about a half hour in advance is okay.

NOTES

These can be made days in advance and kept refrigerated until ready to serve. Everyone likes these for the crunch of the grape and the combination of cheeses and nuts. This is a tidy hors d'oeuvre, since the pretzel keeps guests' fingers from getting sticky. To preserve leftover balls, remove the pretzel sticks before refrigerating. Insert fresh pretzel sticks to serve again.

CHEESE & DEVILED HAM HORS D'OEUVRES

INGREDIENTS

3 ounces cream cheese, softened

2 ounces blue cheese, crumbled

1 can (2 and 1/4 ounces) deviled ham

Several drops of onion juice

1/4 cup ground pecans

1/2 cup snipped fresh parsley

Ground pecans for coating

Chopped pecans for coating

Snipped fresh parsley for coating

Pretzel sticks

PROCEDURE

- Blend the two cheeses, deviled ham, onion juice, ground pecans, and parsley.
- Chill at least one hour.
- Shape into small bite-size balls (a heaping 1/2 teaspoon).
- For a variety of coatings, roll some balls in ground pecans, some in the chopped pecans, and some in the snipped parsley. Those rolled in the ground pecans are the most popular; those rolled in the chopped pecans provide another texture; the ones rolled in parsley add color to the serving plate.
- Refrigerate until ready to serve.
- When ready to serve, insert pretzel stick, holding it at the end so it won't break.

NOTES

Makes 2 to 3 dozen balls. Can be made days in advance of serving. Pretzel sticks should be inserted shortly before ready to serve—no more than half an hour—so they don't get soggy. If there are any leftovers, remove pretzel sticks and refrigerate balls. Insert new pretzel sticks to serve again. This is another great hors d'oeuvre since everything is eaten and there are no messy fingers or leftover toothpicks.

CHEESE SPREAD

INGREDIENTS

2/3 cup cream style cottage cheese OR small curd cottage cheese, creamed

1/2 cup peanut butter (creamy or chunky)

1 tablespoon honey

1/4 cup shredded carrots

2 tablespoons raisins

PROCEDURE

- Combine cottage cheese, peanut butter, and honey and mix well.
- Stir in carrots and raisins.
- To serve, spread on crackers, rice cakes, bagels, toast, or in celery stalks.

NOTES

This is a healthful, simple hors d'oeuvre or snack. Great for the kids but adults love them too.

CHEESE BREAD

INGREDIENTS

3 cups all-purpose flour

1 and 1/2 teaspoons baking soda

1/2 teaspoon salt (add only if using a low-sodium cheddar cheese)

1 and 1/2 cups cheddar cheese, grated

2 eggs

6 tablespoons white vinegar, plus skim milk to make 1 and 1/2 cups liquid

1/4 cup shortening, melted

1 teaspoon caraway seeds (optional)

PROCEDURE

- In medium to large mixing bowl, sift together the flour and baking soda (and salt, if being used).
- Add grated cheese and mix well.
- In separate bowl, beat eggs and add vinegar/milk liquid and melted shortening.
- Stir in caraway seeds (if used).
- Add all at once to flour mixture and mix lightly.
- Pour into greased 9 x 5 loaf pan.
- Bake at 350 degrees for about 1 hour and 10 minutes or until done.
- Remove from pan and cool before serving.

NOTES

Makes about 12 slices.

WISCONSIN BLUE CHEESE CUCUMBER SALAD

INGREDIENTS

2 medium cucumbers, peeled and thinly sliced

Salt

1 medium onion, sliced

1 cup (8 ounces) sour cream

1/2 cup crumbled Wisconsin blue cheese

1/2 teaspoon celery salt

1/4 teaspoon pepper

4 medium tomatoes, sliced

PROCEDURE

- Layer cucumbers in bowl and lightly salt each layer.
- Let stand 30 minutes.
- Drain, rinse, and pat dry.
- Combine with onion slices.
- In separate bowl, combine sour cream, blue cheese, celery salt, and pepper.
- Spoon mixture over cucumbers and onions and toss lightly.
- Serve on plate lined with tomato slices.

NOTES

I presented this salad on one of my *Foods That Made Wisconsin Famous* TV shows—even the burly camera crew liked it.

MACARONI-CHEESE-HAM SALAD

INGREDIENTS

1 cup uncooked macaroni

2 cups diced, cooked ham

1 cup sharp cheddar cheese, cubed

1 cup Swiss cheese, cubed

1 cup diced celery (about 2 stalks)

1 small onion, chopped

1/2 cup chopped sweet pickle

1/2 cup sour cream

2 tablespoons prepared mustard

PROCEDURE

- Cook macaroni according to package instructions.
- In large bowl combine all ingredients except sour cream and mustard.
- In small bowl, mix together the sour cream and mustard.
- Pour over macaroni and mix.
- Chill.

NOTES

A garnish of tomato slices adds color. This recipe won a Blue Ribbon at the Wisconsin State Fair way back in 1958 and is still a favorite, more than 40 years later. Throughout this book are recipes from many years ago, but they have held up with the passages of time and lifestyle changes. The ones I have included are definitely old-time favorites. A tip about cooking macaroni: If you plan to pour a sauce on it, just rinse in hot water. If you plan to bake it in a recipe, just rinse in cold water. The macaroni folks claim that the sauce will adhere better to the macaroni rinsed in hot water; macaroni rinsed in cold water will maintain its "independence" better and not get all coated and mushed up with the other ingredients. I think I'm willing to believe this.

WISCONSIN FARM HOUSE CHEESE SUPPER

INGREDIENTS

1/4 cup beer
1/8 cup unsalted butter
3 tablespoons flour
1/4 teaspoon paprika
Salt/pepper to taste
1/8 teaspoon ground red pepper
1 cup milk
1 cup evaporated milk
1 tablespoon dry mustard
1/2 cup cheddar cheese, shredded
1/2 cup Gouda cheese, shredded
1/2 cup baby Swiss cheese, shredded
1/2 pound cooked, drained (but not rinsed) mostaccioli pasta
1/2 pound smoked ham, cut julienne style OR in chunks
3/4 cups, seeded, diced plum tomatoes
Paprika for garnish

PROCEDURE

- In small saucepan, simmer beer for 3 minutes or until reduced by half and set aside.
- In large saucepan, melt butter.
- Blend in flour, paprika, salt/pepper to taste, and red pepper.
- Cook about 2 minutes, stirring constantly. This mixture is called a roux.
- Gradually add to the roux: milk, evaporated milk, and the beer simmered earlier. Stir until thick.
- Remove from heat and add the dry mustard and the 3 cheeses and stir until all are melted.
- In large bowl, combine mostaccioli, ham, and tomatoes.
- Add cheese sauce and mix.
- Pour into large buttered casserole.
- Bake at 350 degrees for 25 minutes.
- Garnish with paprika.

NOTES

This excellent casserole recipe is from the Wisconsin Milk Marketing Board. I believe it was one of a series of dishes developed for the board by nationally known chefs. It makes a large amount so unless you have a big family or a crowd for supper, you might want to scale it down.

NEVER-FAIL CHEESE SOUFFLÉ

INGREDIENTS

6 tablespoons butter

6 tablespoons flour

1/4 teaspoon salt

1/8 teaspoon pepper

1/4 teaspoon dry mustard

1/8 teaspoon nutmeg

1 and 1/2 cups milk

6 egg yolks, well beaten

1 and 1/2 cups shredded sharp cheddar cheese (use only sharp)

3 tablespoons grated Parmesan cheese

6 egg whites

1/4 teaspoon cream of tartar

PROCEDURE

- In small saucepan, melt butter.
- Stir in flour, salt, pepper, mustard, and nutmeg and cook over medium heat until mixture bubbles.
- Remove from heat and blend in milk.
- Return to burner and cook over medium heat until mixture thickens and bubbles.
- Remove from heat and, in medium-size bowl, beat mixture into egg yolks and slowly add cheeses until melted.
- Cool.
- In large bowl, beat egg whites with cream of tartar until stiff but not dry.
- Gently fold cheese mixture into egg whites.
- Pour into ungreased 8-inch soufflé dish.
- Bake at 350 degrees for 55 minutes or until puffed, golden, and light to the touch.
- Serve at once.

NOTES

Serves 6 to 8. I often add mushrooms or diced ham, but then the soufflé doesn't seem to rise as high. If you want a smaller soufflé and have a 6-inch soufflé dish, reduce portions by half. This really is a "never-fail" recipe. It comes from the Pfaltzgraff Company, the oldest potter in the United States (since 1811).

CHEESE APPLE QUICHE

INGREDIENTS

10-inch unbaked pie crust

7 ounces sharp cheddar cheese, grated

2 tart apples (such as Granny Smith), peeled and sliced

2 tablespoons butter

1 tablespoon sugar

1/4 teaspoon cinnamon

3 eggs

1 and 1/2 cups whipping cream

Grated nutmeg, as needed

PROCEDURE

- Sprinkle cheese over pie crust.
- Sauté apples in butter for about 3 minutes.
- Distribute apples over cheese.
- Mix sugar and cinnamon and sprinkle over apples.
- Whisk eggs and cream.
- Pour into dish.
- Top with grated nutmeg.
- Bake at 375 degrees for 45 minutes.
- Let stand 10 minutes before slicing and serving.

NOTES

Who said real men don't eat quiche? I think they'll like this one.

SOFT CHEESE PRETZELS

INGREDIENTS

1/2 package (1/4 ounce) dry yeast

3/4 cup warm water (hot tap water will do)

1/2 tablespoon sugar

1/4 teaspoon salt

2 cups flour (divided into two 1 cup portions)

1/2 cup sharp cheddar cheese, shredded

1 egg, beaten

Coarse salt

PROCEDURE

- Mix yeast and water.
- Add sugar and salt.
- Gradually add 1 cup flour and beat well with electric mixer.
- With spoon, stir in cheese and remaining 1 cup flour.
- Knead a few minutes to form a soft dough.
- Divide dough into 4 equal portions.
- Roll each portion into strands about 18 inches long and 1/2 inch in diameter.
- Put strands on baking sheet to form a U shape, bring both ends down across bottom of U to make two loops crossing each other, and pinch ends.
- Brush each pretzel with beaten egg and sprinkle with salt.
- Bake at 425 degrees for 10 to 15 minutes or until lightly browned.

NOTES

I think kids should learn to cook and become familiar with kitchen procedures. This is an excellent recipe for a fun family project.

BEER CHEESE FONDUE

INGREDIENTS

2 tablespoons butter, room temperature

1/2 small onion, finely chopped

1 tablespoon Worcestershire sauce

1 teaspoon hot pepper or taco sauce

1/4 teaspoon garlic powder

1 and 1/2 pounds sharp cheddar cheese spread
    (sold in a plastic container as a snack with crackers)

3/4 cup crumbled blue cheese

1/2 to 1 cup beer

Unsliced round loaf of sourdough or other bread (optional)

Vegetables, cut in bite-size pieces (optional)

PROCEDURE

• Melt butter in medium saucepan over medium heat.

• Add onion and sauté until soft.

• Add Worcestershire sauce, pepper or taco sauce, and garlic powder and reduce heat to medium low.

• Add cheddar cheese spread a little at a time to melt.

• Gradually add blue cheese and enough beer for desired consistency.

• Continue to cook until mixture is entirely melted.

• To serve in the round loaf of bread: Cut a thin slice horizontally off the top. With a sharp knife, cut a circle in interior about 1/2 inch from edge. Scoop out interior bread, leaving about 1/2 inch on the bottom. Slice the bread you removed into cubes for dipping.

• Bake hollowed-out bread at 350 for at least 5 minutes to strengthen it.

• Fill bread with the hot fondue.

• Serve with bread cubes or bite-size vegetables.

• When all the fondue is eaten, the bread container can be sliced and eaten. (I actually like this part the best.)

NOTES

While not as popular as it once was, this hot cheese fondue would be a perfect snack to serve while watching a football game in fall or on a snowy winter afternoon.

CREAMY BAKED CHEESECAKE

INGREDIENTS

Crust

1 cup graham cracker crumbs

1/4 cup sugar (I prefer brown to white)

1/4 cup butter, melted

Some cinnamon and ground pecans (I add these to most of my graham cracker crust recipes)

Reserve some crumbs for top

Filling

16 ounces softened cream cheese

1 can (14 ounces) sweetened condensed milk

3 eggs

1/4 teaspoon salt

1/4 cup lemon juice

8 ounces sour cream

PROCEDURE

Crust

• Combine crumbs, sugar, butter, cinnamon, and pecans and pat in bottom of buttered 9-inch springform pan. (Optional: Before I make the bottom crust, I lightly butter the sides of the pan and swirl some plain graham cracker crumbs around the sides.)

Filling

• In large bowl, beat cream cheese until fluffy.

• Add condensed milk, eggs, and salt and beat until smooth.

• Blend in lemon juice.

• Pour into crust.

• Bake at 350 degrees for 50 to 55 minutes until cake springs back when touched (Tip: Since the springform pan might leak, put some foil on the bottom of the oven to catch any drips because they are very difficult to clean up. I have a round metal sheet with a hole in the center, like a donut, which was made for this type of problem. It works great so if you find one, I suggest you buy it.)

• Cool to room temperature.

• Spread sour cream on top.

• Sprinkle with the reserved graham cracker crumbs

• Chill.

NOTES

I heat a knife under hot water before cutting each slice to make nice clean cuts. I shall end this section on cheese with Clifton Fadiman's definition: "Cheese is milk's leap into immortality."

NORTHWOODS
CHAPTER FIVE

FLORENCE

FOREST

IRON

LANGLADE

LINCOLN

MARINETTE

OCONTO

ONEIDA

PRICE

TAYLOR

VILAS

The North Woods is one of Wisconsin's most beautiful areas but it is not renowned for its culinary contributions. It is rich in lumbering, legends, and myths, however, and lumberjack food and lifestyle deserve some attention.

The North Woods region is just that—woods and more woods! Nicolet National Forest, the American Legion State Forest, and two large tracts of Chequamegon National Forest occupy a good portion of the entire region. A third, larger tract is located in Indian Head Country (chapter 6). And among the woods are hundreds of lakes—Vilas County alone has 346 lakes and ponds within its 867 square miles. Early glacial history explains the many isolated landlocked lakes, including the Eagle River chain, which is the longest such chain in the world.

A Paul Bunyan story offers another explanation. It seems the legendary lumberjack jumped from the top of Rib Mountain near Eau Claire in Indian Head Country, and when he landed in a nearby lake, the splashes were so large that the drops created the hundreds of lakes in the North Woods region many, many miles away.

Real life in a lumber camp was anything but glamorous. Imagine the bunkhouse heated by a smoky potbellied stove strewn with drying woolen clothes that filled the air with a sweaty steaminess. Not to mention the less-than-sweet smells coming from the lumberjacks, who generally had no chance to bathe from late fall to early spring. There were no indoor showers and it was just too frigid outside even for a sponge bath.

A historical point of interest: Jefferson Davis, later the president of the Confederacy, has been called the First Lumberman of Wisconsin. He was not a lumberjack, but in 1828 he did command a labor detail for the construction of Fort Winnebago.

Life was hard, and even the diversion of eating was less than enjoyable. The cook (cleverly known as Cookee) was generally the most important person in the camp. Moms of the world take note: No one—absolutely no one—would ever dare to challenge Cookee's menu. Food was plentiful, but it was seldom good. The custom was to have a huge meal of meat, potatoes, and dessert. This was no pot roast with all the trimmings, but rather a hunk of meat and potatoes doused with molasses. Was this to cover up a bad taste or to improve the taste? I prefer my molasses in cookies!

Furthermore, this meal that would hardly win any prizes was eaten in total silence. "Pass the flapjacks," "Give me some red horse [salt beef]," or some such terse phrase were the only utterances permitted. To say anything else might arouse the wrath of Cookee, and any chatterbox who dared speak any more than the essentials might well find himself on the floor. The reason for the enforced silence was to accommodate Cookee, who wanted to get the men out as fast as possible so he could begin to prepare the next meal. Also, the camp bosses figured the faster the men shoveled in the food, the sooner they would get back to work. Two other less obvious but equally important reasons were to discourage fights and possibly squelch any conversations about forming a labor union to improve working conditions, even though lumberjacking was not really a permanent occupation. Most men lasted only one or two of the harsh winters.

Lumbermen stories abound, but here are two of my favorites. Accompanying the lumber rafts floating down the Wisconsin River was a raft called a wanigan that was a floating kitchen. "Wanigan" also referred to a lumberjack's trunk or a lumber camp's supply chest, as well as a small house or lean-to set on wheels or tractor treads and used temporarily as an office or cabin. On one particularly long river trip, Captain John Marshall asked his cook, Whiskey Joe, if he ever used a cookbook. The captain was implying that the unimaginative, repetitious menu could use some variety. Whiskey Joe replied, "Tried it once, but every recipe says, 'Take a clean dish' " — thus revealing his dish-washing habits. The other story involves a French Canadian lumberjack. Like most lumbermen, he could not read or write so when he ordered supplies he drew pictures to convey what he needed. A shipment finally arrived and one of the items was a large round of cheese. He mused to the camp boss, "I no order cheese; I order grindstone." He had forgotten to draw a hole in the crude circle of his pictorial order list.

The North Woods area with its hundreds of lakes is well known the world over for its muskie, pike, and other fishing. It was the fishing playground for the likes of President Eisenhower and Gypsy Rose Lee and is still the fishing paradise for fishermen from all walks of life.

Life in the wilderness, though it was sparsely populated, did not preclude sociability. It was not unusual for travelers to stumble upon a cabin where they were welcome to help themselves in the kitchen even though the owner might be off in the woods. One such traveler had the good fortune to enter a cabin where a great breakfast was available. The coffee seemed to taste different, however, and when he looked in the pot there was a well-cooked, tender frog.

A popular social event where isolated settlers could get together to talk and catch up on news was the donation party. The event generally was held to help out a recent widow. Neighbors brought flour and other staples that she might need for herself and her children.

While game and fish aren't necessarily foods that made Wisconsin famous, they do represent good eatin'. A couple of North Woods specialties are Shoepac Pie, Johnny Cake, and Hodag Pie. Shoepac Pie was haute cuisine in a lumber camp, Johnny Cake was invented out of necessity, and Hodag Pie was created in the fertile mind of a jokester.

SHOEPAC PIE

Dessert (from the French *desservir*, "to clear away") appears when all the dishes have been removed at the end of a meal. Since they are generally delicate in flavor, it almost seems incongruous to serve dessert to hurly-burly lumberjacks. But after the usual hearty meal of meat and potatoes, even a lumberjack appreciated something sweet.

Here's a recipe from cookee Frank Sloup, who joined a logging camp as a cook's helper in the early 1900s. Actually, it's a rather sophisticated recipe, so

Sloup probably had some cooking knowledge before he got to the camp and attempted to feed the boys an untested recipe. My sneaking suspicion is that Cookee knew this pie was basically a butterscotch pie, but that's kind of a sissy-sounding name, isn't it? I imagine he just gave his own "original" recipe creation a name the men could relate to: Shoepac, which is a heavy, laced waterproof boot. It also refers to an Indian moccasin with an extra sole. Maybe Cookee's pie crust tasted like shoe leather—who knows?

SHOEPAC PIE

INGREDIENTS

Filling

4 tablespoons cornstarch

2 tablespoons flour

1/2 teaspoon salt

2 tablespoons white sugar

1/2 cup cold water

3 tablespoons butter

2 cups firmly packed brown sugar

1 and 2/3 cups boiling water

1 teaspoon vanilla

4 egg yolks, slightly beaten (save whites for the meringue)

1 9-inch baked pastry shell

Meringue

4 egg whites

1/4 teaspoon cream of tartar

6 tablespoons sugar

PROCEDURE

Filling

- In small bowl, mix together cornstarch, flour, salt, sugar, 1/2 cup cold water.
- Mix to a smooth paste and set aside.
- In large, heavy saucepan melt butter.
- Add brown sugar and stir over low heat until well blended.
- Add boiling water and vanilla and bring to a boil, stirring constantly.
- Continue to stir until mixture turns a glossy dark brown.
- Slowly add the cornstarch paste that had been set aside to the butter/sugar mixture until it thickens, stirring constantly.
- Gradually stir in the egg yolks.
- Increase heat and cook until thick, stirring constantly.
- Pour into baked pie shell and allow to cool.

Meringue

- Beat egg whites with cream of tartar until frothy.
- Slowly beat in sugar.
- Cover cooled pie with meringue and bake at 250 degrees for about 20 minutes until meringue cooks through.
- Put under broiler until meringue turns golden brown.

JOHNNY CAKE

Johnny Cake is thought to date back to the early 1700s and perhaps was the original pancake. It was a flat griddlecake made of cornmeal, salt, and boiling water or cold milk.

Johnny Cake was also called Shawnee Cake, for the Shawnee Indians who introduced the settlers to cornmeal and cooked it on hot flat stones. Some sources say the original name for Johnny Cake in America was Journey Cake. The word *journey* used to refer to the distance that one could travel in one day's time. It was the original flatbread variety that itinerant preachers and other travelers carried because it traveled well and kept for a long time.

Later when other ingredients—eggs, shortening, and baking power—were added and the mixture was baked in the oven, it became a cake-like cornbread rather than a flatbread. It was also called hoecake because workers who did the hoeing took it to the fields and also because the person who cooked the bread used the metal edge of a hoe to keep it in place on the griddle.

JOHNNY CAKE

INGREDIENTS

1 cup cornmeal

1 teaspoon salt

2/3 cup sugar (if a sweeter cake is desired, add 2 tablespoons brown sugar)

1 cup sifted flour

1 teaspoon baking powder

3/4 teaspoon baking soda

2 eggs beaten

1/4 cup butter, melted

1 and 1/4 cups buttermilk (make your own by adding 1 teaspoon vinegar OR 2 teaspoons lemon juice to 1 cup milk for each cup needed).

PROCEDURE

- In medium to large bowl, stir together the dry ingredients.
- In separate bowl, beat eggs, butter, and buttermilk.
- Combine liquid and dry ingredients.
- Put in greased 9 x 9 inch pan.
- Bake at 425 degrees for 25 minutes.

NOTES

If you want to use this as a dessert, do what the lumbermen did and douse each piece of cake with maple syrup.

HODAG PIE

Lumberjack lore tells of the Hudag, a huge moose-like animal that had jointless legs and had to sleep propped up against a tree. Few actually ever saw the Hudag but liquor improved the chances that one indeed would see it!

Not to be outdone, in 1896 near Rhinelander, Eugene Shepard said he had captured a Hodag (remarkably similar spelling) and put it to death in its cave. Supposedly, the Hodag was a terrible animal that roamed the woods. It had the body of an ox, the tail of an alligator, two horns on its head and twelve on its back, and it ate white bulldogs—but only on Sunday. Of course, it breathed fire and had two different colored eyes (who could ever get that close to notice?). The prestigious Smithsonian Institution supposedly even sent a scientist to investigate.

Rhinelander became known as the Home of the Hodag. Trouble is, a few years after the Hodag's capture and demise, Shepard admitted that the story was a hoax. No kidding!

But the story was an entrepreneur's dream (not to mention an enthusiastic chamber of commerce). One Rhinelander restaurant created the concoction that follows and named it after Shepard's fantasy. Believe me, you won't find this recipe in any other cookbook.

HODAG PIE

INGREDIENTS

1 9-inch unbaked pastry shell

1 and 1/2 cups grated cheddar cheese (divide into 1 cup and 1/2 cup portions)

2/3 cup diced cooked chicken or turkey

2 eggs

1/2 cup finely minced onion

1 cup sour cream

1/3 cup mayonnaise

1/2 teaspoon Worcestershire sauce

1 to 2 cups chopped broccoli (if fresh, blanch; if frozen, thaw)

PROCEDURE

- Sprinkle 1/2 cup cheese over bottom of pastry shell.
- Top with chicken or turkey.
- In medium bowl, beat eggs.
- Stir in onion, sour cream, mayonnaise, and Worcestershire sauce.
- Pour mixture over the chicken or turkey.
- Cover with broccoli and the remaining 1 cup of cheese.
- Bake at 425 degrees for 30 to 45 minutes or until lightly browned.

NOTES

The owner of the Rhinelander restaurant was clever to capitalize on the Hodag name, but the ingredients of this recipe sound like the makings of a chicken pot pie!

FISH

Wisconsin's lakes and rivers annually attract well over 100,000 fishermen, and one of their greatest challenges is the muskie (short for muskellunge), the state fish. Boulder Junction in Vilas County is the Muskie Capital of the World, a designation awarded by the U.S. Patent Office in 1971 for its high muskie catch. Wisconsin has more than seven hundred muskie lakes—two hundred of them within a nine-mile radius of Boulder Junction—and more than forty muskie streams. The very largest muskies weigh seventy pounds, and the female muskie usually is heavier than the male.

The National Fresh Water Fishing Hall of Fame in Hayward (in Sawyer County in Indian Head Country) has a four-story concrete muskie with gaping jaws where many a tourist has had her picture taken.

One of the most popular eating fish is the walleye pike, although it's not really a pike but a member of the perch family. Its delicate meat is white and flaky and delicious no matter how prepared—poached, grilled, or fried. Walleyes are common throughout Wisconsin lakes and rivers, and the best time to catch them is on cloudy days or evenings when the fish move from the deeper to the shallower waters. They favor reefs, rocky shores, and sandy bottoms and the best bait is a minnow (three to four inches) or a nightcrawler attached to a weighted jig hook. Another tip: Walleyes travel in schools, so if you're lucky enough to catch one, keep fishing the same area.

Wisconsin has a huge variety of other fish—bass, trout, and countless pan fish to satisfy anglers and their appetites. But fish farming (especially trout) is a rapidly growing Wisconsin business. It ensures uncontaminated fish and provides a consistent and more mild flavor than that of stream-caught trout.

People fish for fun and not for survival, and it has been said that if one wants to stimulate the imagination, try fishing. Another wise person said, "Many a problem will solve itself if we forget it and go fishing."

FRIDAY NIGHT FISH FRY

INGREDIENTS

Perch fillets

Beer (not "lite" variety), as needed to cover fillets

7-Up soda, as needed to cover fillets

Seasoned bread crumbs

Vegetable oil for frying

PROCEDURE

- Marinate perch in a combination of the beer and 7-Up (equal portions) for at least half an hour.
- Remove from marinade and rinse the fillets 3 or 4 times to remove any obvious fish or beer taste.
- Pat dry.
- Pat by hand the seasoned bread crumbs into the fillets, pressing firmly into the fish.
- Place breaded fillets on tray, cover, and refrigerate overnight.
- When ready to serve, deep fry in oil until golden and done; may be fried in a deep skillet.

NOTES

Fish fries are a Friday night tradition, and many country taverns or neighborhood bars make a reputation for themselves with their fish fry plates. The fish was almost always perch but now, because of shortages, haddock or cod is often substituted. Taverns and restaurants generally buy prebreaded fish from their suppliers, but a small tavern/restaurant in Elkhart Lake prepares its perch from start to finish and this is their recipe. I was so impressed with the delicate coating and nongreasy taste that I featured its cook on my TV cooking show, The *Foods That Made Wisconsin Famous*. The perch should be served with the traditional cole slaw, buttered rye bread, and German potato salad.

PAN-FRIED FISH

INGREDIENTS

Any variety pan fish, cleaned (approximately 4 fillets)
1 tablespoon lemon juice
1/2 cup cream
Vegetable oil for frying, if needed

PROCEDURE

- Place fish in heavy skillet over medium high heat.
- Add oil, if needed (see Notes).
- Mix lemon juice and cream .
- Spread mixture on fish two or three times while cooking.

NOTES

The secret to deliciously browned, pan-fried fish is "dry heat"; this means using very little fat in the pan. Some fish are fattier than others (whitefish, trout), so any fat should be poured off as it accumulates. Fish with less fat may be improved by basting, and the above two simple ingredients work just fine.

BAKED MUSKIE

INGREDIENTS

4 pounds muskie

2 cups cold water

6 carrot slices

6 onion slices

Small bunch parsley

6 crushed peppercorns

1/2 teaspoon salt

1/2 cup butter

3 tablespoons flour

1 and 1/2 tablespoons lemon juice

1/2 tablespoon finely chopped chives

Salt

A few grains cayenne pepper

3/4 cup heavy cream

2 tablespoons pimento purée (see notes)

3/4 cup buttered coarse bread crumbs

PROCEDURE

- Cut skinned, boned fish into individual serving sizes.
- Cover the bones, skin, and any trimmings with cold water.
- Add carrot and onion slices, parsley, peppercorns, and salt.
- Bring to boil and simmer until reduced to 1/2 volume.
- Strain mixture and set aside.
- In medium saucepan, melt butter.
- Add flour and blend thoroughly.
- Add strained fish stock and bring to a boil.
- Arrange fish pieces in bottom of a well-buttered baking dish.
- Brush fish fillets with lemon juice, sprinkle each with chopped chives and salt and cayenne pepper to taste.
- Pour boiled fish stock over the top.
- Cover with foil.
- Bake at 375 degrees for 20 minutes.
- Mix pimento purée with cream and heat.
- Pour cream mixture over fish.
- Cover with bread crumbs.
- Drizzle with melted butter.
- Return to oven and bake until browned.

NOTES

To make the pimento purée, simply drain a can of pimentos and put through a fine sieve or puree the pimentos in a blender.

GRILLED AMARETTO-BASTED WALLEYE

INGREDIENTS

4 walleye fillets, 6 to 8 ounces each

1/2 cup (1 stick) butter

2 tablespoons sliced almonds

2 tablespoons Amaretto liqueur

PROCEDURE

- Sauté almonds in butter until lightly browned (this doesn't take long so watch what you're doing).
- Add Amaretto.
- Put mixture in small bowl.
- Place walleye fillets on greased grill.
- Grill over hot coals for four to five minutes on each side.
- Baste with the butter/almond/Amaretto mixture.
- Serve fillets directly from the grill.
- Spoon on remaining butter/almond/Amaretto mixture.

NOTES

If you don't want to grill the fish, you can make it on the stove in a heavy, greased skillet.

POACHED LAKE TROUT

INGREDIENTS

Fish

3 to 4 pounds lake trout, cut into fillets

1/2 cup milk

1/2 cup water

4 slices lemon

1/2 teaspoon allspice

1/2 teaspoon salt

1 sprig parsley

White Sauce

2 tablespoons butter

2 tablespoons all-purpose flour

1 cup milk

1/4 teaspoon salt

1/8 teaspoon pepper

1 and 1/2 tablespoons lemon juice

2 hard-cooked eggs, chopped

PROCEDURE

Fish

- Combine milk, water, lemon slices, allspice, salt, parsley.
- Place fish in skillet.
- Pour liquid mixture over fish.
- Cover and cook over low heat for 20 minutes until tender.
- Carefully remove fish to hot platter.

White Sauce

- In medium saucepan, melt butter.
- Blend in flour thoroughly.
- Add milk, salt, pepper.
- Bring to boil, stirring constantly, until thickened.
- Combine hot white sauce, lemon juice, and chopped eggs.
- Pour hot sauce over fish and serve.

GAME

The term *game* applies to wild animals that are deemed suitable for human consumption. The most common large game in Wisconsin is the deer. Small game includes pheasant, rabbit, squirrel, duck, and wild turkey.

Hunting in Wisconsin usually means deer hunting. Workplace attendance drops, wives are temporarily widowed, and the whole state seems to be consumed in "the hunt." A common highway scene in November is a deer strapped to the car roof and perhaps a fresh spruce tree as well, for the coming Christmas season. As long as one is in the woods, why not pick up a tree too?

Hundreds of thousands of deer are "harvested" (a gentler word than shot and killed, right?) each season with guns, and as many as 70,000 more deer by intrepid hunters with bow and arrow.

Originally, venison (from the Latin *venatio*, "hunting") referred to any kind of wild game, but now it almost always means deer meat. Venison can be prepared in many ways, but first-time cooks would be well advised to refer to a game cookbook.

What was once survival food is now sometimes a sophisticated finger food. I'm referring to Venison Jerky, the word *jerky* coming from a Spanish word for sun-dried meat. Dry it in the sun if you wish, but I recommend the following modern-day oven-dried version from my son-in-law, Bob. Originally from Alaska, Bob lived in Northern Wisconsin for a while, and is now back in Alaska. Boy, can he hunt up there!

I suggest that first-time cooks also refer to a game cookbook when preparing small game such as pheasant. Or perhaps you want to do as Native Americans did. They cleaned (and sometimes plucked) pigeons, rabbits, and other small game and then covered the animal or bird in clay. They made holes in the clay to allow steam to escape and placed it in the firepit to bake. At the appropriate time (they knew when), they removed the clay. If they hadn't removed the hair or feathers, most of it came off easily because it stuck to the clay. On second thought, maybe it's just easier to find a restaurant that serves game. Agreed?

VENISON JERKY

INGREDIENTS

1 pound venison steak cut into long thin strips

1 tablespoon black pepper

1 and 1/2 tablespoons salt

1 tablespoon onion powder

4 tablespoons dried brown sugar (to dry, let sugar sit out overnight OR place in a dish in a very low heated oven for a few minutes OR run sugar through a coffee grinder, which aerates the sugar and dries it out). It is essential that the sugar be dried so that the mixture can be easily sprinkled on the meat.

PROCEDURE

- Mix pepper, salt, onion powder, and dried brown sugar to shaker consistency (it should be both salty and sweet—add additional pepper or salt to taste).Sprinkle liberally on both sides of each strip of meat.
- Insert toothpick near the top of each strip of meat.
- Hang meat so that the toothpick rests on the highest oven rack and the meat hangs freely below (place aluminum foil on oven bottom to catch drips).
- Bake at 200 degrees for 4 to 5 hours.
- Meat will appear dried and darkened and slightly hard to the touch.
- Leave meat in oven overnight.
- In the morning, remove meat from oven, remove toothpicks, and store in airtight container.

HOT VENISON SPREAD

INGREDIENTS

1 pound ground venison

1/2 cup onion, chopped

1/4 cup green pepper, chopped

1 clove garlic, minced

1 tablespoon chili powder

1 teaspoon cumin

1/3 teaspoon cayenne pepper

2 tablespoons ketchup

1 can (16 ounces) refried beans, mashed

Oil for browning meat

PROCEDURE

- In large skillet, brown meat, onion, green pepper, and garlic.
- Remove from heat and place in large mixing bowl.
- Add chili powder, cumin, cayenne pepper, and ketchup.
- Add beans to meat mixture and blend thoroughly.
- Serve warm on crackers.

NOTES

If you want it spicier, add more cayenne pepper. Keeps in refrigerator for up to a week or may be frozen for months. Reheats well in microwave.

VENISON WITH BREAD DUMPLINGS

INGREDIENTS

Venison
2 pounds venison, sliced
Water as needed
2 teaspoons salt
4 bay leaves
1 teaspoon black pepper
1 onion, sliced
1 tablespoon shortening
2 large onions, diced
2 ounces dry red wine (optional, but I wouldn't skip it!)
1/8 teaspoon baking soda
2 tablespoons flour
1 pint sour cream
1/2 teaspoon vinegar

Bread Dumplings
4 eggs
4 cups all-purpose flour
1 teaspoon salt
3/4 cup water
10 slices bread
1 tablespoon shortening

PROCEDURE

Venison
- Place meat in large glass bowl with enough water to cover.
- Add salt, bay leaves, pepper, and the 1 sliced onion.
- Let stand overnight; next day, drain water and rinse meat.
- In large skillet, melt shortening, add diced onion, and brown.
- Add meat, a little salt, black pepper, and wine and simmer until almost all of the juice is gone.
- Slowly add enough hot water to cover meat.
- Add baking soda, and simmer until meat is done.
- Mix flour and sour cream; slowly add to meat and simmer until well blended.
- Add vinegar.

Bread Dumplings
- In large bowl, mix eggs, flour, salt, and beat with spoon, adding enough water so dough is quite soft.
- Cut off bottom hard crust of bread and discard; cube bread.
- In skillet, melt shortening and brown the bread; set aside to cool.
- When cool, add to flour/egg dough and let stand 1/2 hour.
- Drop batter by tablespoon into boiling water, cook 20 minutes, and drain.

NOTES

A Hungarian friend gave me this authentic family recipe. Its Hungarian name is *Vadas Hus Kenyer Gombocal*.

ORIGINAL BRUNSWICK STEW

INGREDIENTS

1 squirrel (see Notes)
2 large onions, sliced
2 cups okra, sliced
4 cups tomatoes
2 cups lima beans
3 medium potatoes, diced
4 cups corn
3 teaspoons salt
1 teaspoon pepper
1 tablespoon sugar
3 quarts water

PROCEDURE

- Cut squirrel and simmer in water for about 2 and 1/4 hours.
- Remove, bone, and cut meat into chunks.
- Add raw vegetables and simmer uncovered until tender.

NOTES

Supposedly, this stew originated at a Brunswick County, Virginia, estate where a hunting party was taking place. The cook was supposed to have dinner ready when the group returned; he had the vegetables but no meat, and he didn't want to hunt too far to get it. The only thing he could find nearby was a squirrel. When he served the stew, the hunting party agreed that the squirrel was indeed the tenderest of all wild meats. For a modern-day Brunswick Stew (unless you want to hunt for squirrel), a grocery store chicken may be substituted.

PHEASANT

INGREDIENTS

Pheasant, cut up
1 egg
Seasoned bread crumbs or crushed corn flakes, mixed with grated Parmesan cheese
Oil

PROCEDURE

- Dip pheasant pieces into egg.
- Coat with crumb mixture.
- Place pheasant pieces in baking dish with oil.
- Bake at 350 degrees approximately 1 hour (it may be done earlier, so it is best to check after about 20 to 30 minutes of baking, and turn the pieces at that time).

NOTES

I have never made pheasant, but my wife's cousin supplied this recipe. She cooked many, many pheasants, squirrels, rabbits, and other critters since her husband was a true Wisconsin hunter. To complete this section on game, here is a recipe for either squirrel or rabbit (again, from my wife's cousin):

- Cut squirrel or rabbit into joints.
- In large kettle, add bay leaf and enough salted water to cover meat.
- Simmer 20 to 30 minutes or until tender.
- Remove and brown in fry pan.
- Salt/pepper to taste.

INDIAN HEAD COUNTRY
CHAPTER SIX

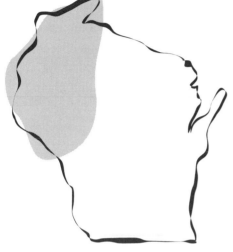

ASHLAND

BARRON

BAYFIELD

BUFFALO

BURNETT

CHIPPEWA

CLARK

DOUGLAS

DUNN

EAU CLAIRE

JACKSON

PEPIN

PIERCE

POLK

RUSK

SAWYER

ST. CROIX

TREMPLEAU

WASHBURN

Indian Head Country is the largest of the six designated regions of Wisconsin, covering almost the entire northwestern part of the state. It has a rich Indian history and is noted for three important foods: wild rice, turkey, and horseradish. Like the North Woods, it has hundreds of lakes, as well as the National Fresh Water Fishing Hall of Fame in Hayward (Sawyer County).

Wild rice (*zizania aquatica*) is also called Indian rice, Tuscarora rice, and Canadian rice. It actually is not a true rice but the grain of a tall aquatic grass. The Indians called it *Manomin* or *Meneninee*, and the Menominee Indians became known as "People of the Wild Rice." The Chippewa Indians called wild rice the "good berry," the French called it "crazy oats," and American settlers called it "water oats" or "water rice."

Today wild rice is cultivated in areas it had never grown in before, but Rice Lake in Barron County still has one of the best "natural" wild rice stands in the world. You don't have to guess where *that* lake got its name. The method of harvesting has not changed. Harvesters paddle canoes through dense rice fields and use a pole to pull the growth above water toward the canoe and then whack it so the rice falls into the bottom of the canoe. Never mind that some goes back into the water since that merely seeds the field for another season. This hand method of reaping, as well as the need for the proper growing area, accounts for the price of wild rice. However, one pound (approximately 2 and 2/3 cups) makes thirty servings. Basically, wild rice is prepared like other kinds of rice but it does take a little longer to cook.

The Turkey Capital of Wisconsin is Barron, a town in the midst of many turkey farms. Some say the word *turkey* is a corruption of the Indian name for that bird, *furkee*.

Benjamin Franklin said the national bird should be the turkey rather than the bald eagle because in his mind the turkey was "a true original

177

native of America." It's not even certain how the turkey came to be associated with Thanksgiving, which the pilgrims first celebrated in New England in 1621. Wild turkey authority A. W. Schorger claims that "turkey was not necessarily served" at the feast. I still like the idea that it was served—after all, wild turkeys were in the area and a plump turkey does serve a big crowd.

While not a memorable political sound bite, the first official association between Thanksgiving and turkey came from Alexander Hamilton when he purportedly said, "No citizen of the U.S. should refrain from eating turkey on Thanksgiving Day."

Horseradish in its raw state resembles a horse's hoof—hence, the less-than-inspired name. It's frequently used in making pickles and added to mustards and seafood sauce. Elkis Huntsinger, a farmer near Eau Claire, objected to having to grate the root at every meal (or so the story goes). One morning he accidentally spilled cream into his bowl of freshly grated horseradish. A bit disgusted with this mess, he left the table and let it sit until the noon meal. Rather than throwing it out, he tasted it and found that it was still "hot." Thus were horseradish sauces invented—eventually.

Indian tribes existed not only in Indian Head Country but throughout Wisconsin They practiced agriculture, especially the growing of corn, beans, squash, and tobacco—the first three being categorized as the Indian triad. They also hunted and they taught early settlers to hunt, a skill they lacked because hunting was reserved exclusively for the aristocracy in England.

Hospitality was a cardinal tenet of Indians. They shared with family, friends, and strangers and often entertained lavishly. They had no written language so orators and singers kept their legends and traditions alive. French explorers and trappers often married Indians, but usually just for one season—they simply gave their brides some gifts. However, after three seasons, they were expected to keep their wives for life. If they did in fact marry, they went to Mackinac (Capital of the West) and a priest would marry them and baptize their children.

Sometimes Indians tried to drive off settlers by destroying their crops before they could be harvested, usually after the first frost, when the weather turned mild again for a short time. Therefore this time of year became known as Indian Summer. Now, of course, we use that same phrase to describe that mild time when all the leaves are in glorious color.

WILD RICE

Wild rice has been called the caviar of grain, probably because of its unique, nutty flavor, crunchy texture, and cost.

Wild rice can be served plain with butter, salt, and pepper or as an accompaniment or bed for poultry, meats, seafood, and fish. It can be used in dishes that call for other types of rice or noodles. Adding it to batters and doughs gives pancakes, waffles, and muffins a different and delightful flavor. It's also a hearty addition to soups and stews.

Nutritionally, wild rice is near ideal. High in complex carbohydrates, it also has 12 to 15 percent protein, less than 1 percent fat, and no cholesterol. It is much higher than other grains in riboflavin, thiamin, and niacin.

The Chieftain Wild Rice Company in Spooner (Washburn County) provides the basic preparation procedures (each method will yield four or more cups cooked wild rice):

STOVETOP METHOD: Wash 1 cup uncooked wild rice thoroughly. Add 3 and 1/2 cups water, salted to taste, in heavy saucepan. Bring water to boil, stir, reduce heat and simmer covered 40 to 45 minutes or just until the rice kernels puff open. Uncover and fluff with table fork. For a chewier texture, reduce cooking time.

OVEN METHOD: Wash 1 cup uncooked wild rice thoroughly. Combine with 3 and 1/2 cups water in a covered 2-quart casserole. Cover and bake at 350 degrees for 1 hour. Check the rice and add more water if needed and fluff with a fork. Continue baking for 1/2 hour. Wild rice should be moist, not dry.

MICROWAVE METHOD: Wash 1 cup uncooked wild rice thoroughly. Combine with 3 and 1/2 cups water in a covered 2-quart casserole. Microwave on high for 5 minutes. Then microwave on medium (50 percent power) for 30 minutes. Let stand 10 to 15 minutes. Drain.

If a recipe calls for sautéing or baking uncooked wild rice with a main entree, simply wash the wild rice thoroughly with warm tap water, rinse, and drain in a strainer until the water runs clear and then soak in salted water several hours or overnight.

Cooked wild rice can be frozen, in a sealed plastic bag, for up to one year. Just thaw when ready to use.

I previously mentioned how wild rice is still harvested in some areas. Obviously, this traditional method has some commercial limitations. Wisconsin's Chieftain Wild Rice Company grows its rice on 300 acres devoted exclusively to wild rice culture. It manages the growth from seed to harvest, then cures and roasts the rice to its own specifications. To ensure the high grade and maintain consistent quality, it does not collect wild rice from other growers or brokers. In addition to 100 percent wild rice, Chieftain also produces a variety of blends with other rices, wheats, and even carrots and celery.

WILD RICE SOUP

INGREDIENTS

2 tablespoons chopped onion

3 tablespoons chopped mushrooms

3 tablespoons butter

1/4 cup flour

4 cups chicken stock (chicken soup base works fine)

Dash salt

1/2 cup cooked wild rice

1 cup half and half cream

1/4 cup sherry

Chopped parsley

PROCEDURE

- In large kettle, cook onions and mushrooms in butter until onion is transparent.
- Add flour and cook 15 minutes.
- Add chicken stock and cook 8 to 10 minutes, stirring until smooth.
- Add salt.
- Add rice, cream, and sherry, and stir until heated through.
- Garnish with freshly chopped parsley.

NOTES

While Wisconsin harvests a good deal of wild rice, Minnesota leads in its production. Rudy Perpich, who was governor of Minnesota from 1983 to 1991, provided this recipe. Governor and Mrs. Perpich served this soup in the executive mansion.

WILD RICE HAM SALAD

INGREDIENTS

1 cup wild rice

1/2 of a 10-ounce package of frozen peas

1/3 cup chopped dill pickle

2/3 cup cooked ham, cubed

2/3 cup mild cheddar cheese, cubed

2 hard-cooked eggs, chopped

1/2 cup mayonnaise

Lettuce, for serving, if desired

PROCEDURE

- Cook the wild rice.
- Chill.
- Cook peas per package instructions.
- In medium to large bowl, combine wild rice, peas, and pickle.
- Mix lightly and chill.
- Before serving, add ham, cheese, and mayonnaise and combine.
- Top with chopped hard-cooked eggs.
- If desired, serve on a lettuce leaf or shredded lettuce.

NOTES

This recipe and the wild rice recipes that follow came from the Chieftain Wild Rice Company of Hayward, Wisconsin.

WILD RICE HAMBURGER CASSEROLE

INGREDIENTS

2/3 cup uncooked wild rice

4 cups cold water, with 1 teaspoon salt

4 ounces fresh mushrooms, sliced, OR 1 can (4 ounces) mushroom pieces, drained

1 medium onion, diced

1 cup celery, thinly sliced

3 tablespoons butter

1 pound ground chuck

1/4 cup flour

1 can (10 and 1/2 ounces) beef broth (you may use a beef soup base)

1/2 teaspoon ground marjoram

1/2 teaspoon salt

1/4 teaspoon dried thyme leaves

PROCEDURE

- Cook wild rice.
- In large skillet, melt butter, and cook mushrooms, onion, and celery over medium heat until tender (about 3 minutes).
- Add ground chuck and cook until meat is brown (about 10 minutes).
- Sprinkle flour on mixture and stir until evenly coated.
- Stir in remaining ingredients.
- Heat to boiling and reduce heat to medium.
- Cook until mixture thickens, stirring constantly.
- Stir in cooked rice and heat until hot.
- Serve from skillet or place in casserole.

NOTES

If desired, cover casserole and place in 300 degree oven to keep it hot. Can be kept in oven for up to 1 hour.

STIR-FRY WILD RICE
SNOW PEAS & PORK

INGREDIENTS

1/2 pound pork tenderloin, sliced 1/4 inch thick

3 tablespoons vegetable oil

1 cup sliced celery

1 cup sliced green onion

1 cup sliced fresh mushrooms

1 can (8 ounces) water chestnuts, sliced

1/2 pound snow peas OR edible pod peas (fresh or frozen, thawed)

1 tablespoon grated fresh ginger root

2 cups cooked wild rice

1 tablespoon cornstarch

1 tablespoon dry sherry

1 teaspoon soy sauce

1/2 teaspoon salt

1/2 teaspoon salted cashews OR sunflower nuts

PROCEDURE

- In heavy skillet, add oil and pork and stir-fry over high heat for 2 minutes or until meat is no longer pink
- Add celery, green onion, mushrooms, water chestnuts, snow peas or pea pods, and ginger and stir-fry for 5 minutes over high heat until vegetables are tender crisp.
- Toss in the wild rice until evenly blended.
- In small bowl, mix cornstarch, sherry, soy sauce, and salt.
- Add to juices in pan and cook until thickened.
- Toss mixture together to coat everything with glaze.
- Garnish with the cashews or sunflower nuts.

WILD RICE CHICKEN CASSEROLE

INGREDIENTS

2/3 cup uncooked wild rice

4 cups cold water with 1 teaspoon salt

1/2 cup butter

1/2 cup flour

2 and 1/2 teaspoons salt

1/4 teaspoon pepper

1 and 1/2 cups chicken broth (you may use a chicken soup base)

2 and 1/4 cups milk

3 cups cubed cooked chicken (or turkey)

1 can (4 ounces) mushrooms, drained and sliced

1/2 of a 4-ounce jar of pimentos, drained and sliced

1/2 cup diced green pepper

1/3 cup slivered almonds

Parsley, minced, for garnish, if desired

PROCEDURE

- Cook the wild rice.
- In large skillet, melt butter; blend in flour, salt, and pepper.
- Cook until mixture is smooth and bubbly, stirring constantly.
- Remove from heat.
- Stir in chicken broth and milk.
- Return to heat and bring to a boil, stirring constantly, about 1 minute.
- Add cooked rice and remaining ingredients.
- Pour into a greased 13 x 9 baking dish.
- Bake at 350 degrees for 40 to 45 minutes.
- If desired, sprinkle with parsley before serving.

HORSERADISH

In 1500 B.C. Grecians treated lower back pain with ground horseradish. Medieval physicians prescribed it for scurvy, tuberculosis, and other such diseases. Mohican Indians used it to treat toothaches. Gypsies used the leaves to combat food poisoning. It is one of the "five bitter herbs" Jews were instructed to eat at Passover. But it was the Germans who discovered how the white, pungent, spicy root embellished the taste of certain foods. The spiky green leaves can be used in salads, but usually one finds only the roots at the grocery store. Horseradish is a member of the mustard family. The Japanese version is *wasabi* or *wasabe*. Its bite and aroma are almost absent until the root is grated or ground and the root's oils are released. The flavor is stabilized with the addition of vinegar and the sooner it is added the milder it is.

Bottled horseradish is available white (preserved in vinegar) or red (preserved in beet juice). Dried horseradish must be reconstituted before using. When you buy horseradish read the label to see if it has been "cut" with turnips or parsnips—it will be milder but might be somewhat tasteless. Nutritionally it has no disadvantages: one tablespoon of prepared horseradish contains no fat, only six calories, and a modest amount of sodium, and it is high in vitamin C and potassium. Therefore, it is a very tasty addition to low-fat dishes. Horseradish should be stored in a tightly covered jar in the refrigerator. Since oxidation is its enemy (causing discoloration) it is best to keep the horseradish jar completely filled with vinegar or lemon juice. Horseradish is especially good with roast beef, but should never be smeared on other meats because it will destroy the aromatics. One of the largest horseradish farms (about eight hundred acres) is located in Eau Claire County and produces about 25 percent of all the horseradish in the United States.

HORSERADISH
SAUCE #1

INGREDIENTS

3 tablespoons butter
3 tablespoons flour
1 and 1/2 cups boiling beef stock (a beef soup base is okay)
Grated horseradish to taste

PROCEDURE

- In small skillet, melt butter.
- Add flour and stir with whisk until blended.
- Add the beef stock all at once and stir vigorously until mixture is smooth and thick.
- Blend in grated horseradish.

NOTES

Makes about 1 and 1/2 cups. To serve with pork, add applesauce to the sauce. To serve with beef, combine 2 to 3 tablespoons of the sauce with 1 cup heavy cream.

HORSERADISH
SAUCE #2

INGREDIENTS

1 cup applesauce

1 tablespoon horseradish (preferably freshly grated)

1 teaspoon Hungarian paprika

PROCEDURE

- Blend all ingredients.

NOTES

This recipe from New York's Colony Restaurant (a very fancy place!) is served with cold, skinned, smoked trout fillets. The Colony makes a special sauce by folding 1 tablespoon of freshly grated horseradish into a cup of whipped cream with some lemon juice and salt added just before serving. Grated horseradish is also delicious when blended with cool, finely grated beets.

TURKEY

Wisconsin ranks tenth in turkey production with about 8.4 million of the 300 million birds grown in the entire country. At least 40 percent of all households serve turkey on a regular basis, largely because it is inexpensive and very healthful. It is low in fat, low in calories and cholesterol, and high in protein. Israel has the highest annual per capita consumption of turkey, and the United States is second (18 pounds).

You've probably heard the phrase, "Let's talk turkey." To me, it's fascinating to learn the origin of such expressions. Seems a white man was hunting with an Indian, and when it came time to divide what they had gathered, the white man said, "I'll give you a choice—you take the buzzard and I'll take the turkey, or I'll take the turkey and you take the buzzard." The Indian knew he was being taken advantage of and replied, "You never once talked turkey to me."

When settlers arrived in America they saw a wild fowl that reminded them of the turkey cocks and hens they had seen in Europe so they just named these wild birds "turkey." The name appears in the writings of Captain John Smith as early as 1607. However, it was discovered later that the native North American turkey (*Meleagris gallopavo*) was a species totally different from the European turkey. Habits are hard to break so they just continued to call these wild birds turkeys, and maybe the Indian name *furkee*, as I mentioned earlier, reinforced the word.

Even a first-time cook should have no trouble roasting a turkey. The instructions that come with frozen turkeys are easy to follow, and the little thermometer that pops out when the turkey is done makes the timing fool-proof. The popularity of turkey has brought a wide variety of turkey choices beyond the whole bird itself. One can buy just the breast, cutlets, tenderloins, thighs, wings, a boneless roast of both white and dark meats, and ground turkey.

Raw turkey meat cooks very quickly because today's breeds have a relatively high protein and low fat composition. Turkey is likened to other quick-cooking foods, such as fish. To ensure rapid cooking and prevent seepage of natural juices, one should preheat the pan or oven before adding turkey cuts. Raw turkey meat should be cooked until it is *just done* and no more. Trust the cooking instructions on the package.

A little turkey trivia:

• Neil Armstrong's and Edwin Aldrin's first meal on the moon was a food packet of roasted turkey.

• Only tom turkeys (males) gobble; hen turkeys (females) make a clicking noise.

• Turkeys can fly for short distances and can run as fast as twenty-five miles per hour. (Might come in handy at Thanksgiving time, right?)

• It's estimated that turkeys have approximately 3,500 feathers at maturity. (Now isn't that a fascinating item for cocktail party conversation?)

• June is Turkey Lovers Month. (probably the best time for turkeys too with Thanksgiving a long way off)

TURKEY JOES

INGREDIENTS

1/2 pound ground turkey
1/2 medium onion, chopped
1/2 cup barbecue sauce
1/2 tablespoon sweet pickle relish
Hamburger buns

PROCEDURE

- In medium size skillet, brown turkey and onion over medium heat until turkey is no longer pink.
- Stir in barbecue sauce and pickle relish.
- Cook 2 to 3 minutes longer to heat thoroughly.
- Serve on buns.

Microwave Version
- Combine turkey and onion in 2-quart casserole.
- Cover with wax paper and microwave on high 2 minutes.
- Stir and microwave another 3 minutes.
- Add barbecue sauce and relish.
- Microwave another minute.

NOTES

This is similar to hamburger sloppy joes. At first glance, it doesn't look terribly exciting, but when I prepared it on my *Foods That Made Wisconsin Famous* TV show the crew and staff all agreed it was very good despite its simplicity.

TURKEY FAJITAS

INGREDIENTS

1 tablespoon Worcestershire sauce

1 tablespoon soy sauce

1 tablespoon vinegar

1 teaspoon chili powder

1 garlic clove, minced

Dash of hot pepper sauce OR ground red pepper

Salt to taste

1 and 1/2 pounds fresh turkey breast, steaks, or split tenderloin

1 to 2 tablespoons oil

1 medium onion, sliced

1 green pepper, sliced

1/2 lemon

4 flour tortillas

PROCEDURE

- In wok or electric skillet, mix together oil, Worcestershire sauce, and soy sauce.
- Add vinegar, chili powder, garlic, hot pepper sauce, and salt.
- Add turkey and vegetables.
- Stir fry until turkey is no longer pink and vegetables are tender.
- Squeeze lemon juice over turkey and vegetables just before serving.
- Serve with tortillas.

APPLE-STUFFED TURKEY TENDERLOIN

INGREDIENTS

1 medium apple, peeled, cored, and diced

1/2 cup orange juice

1/4 cup jellied cranberry sauce

2 tablespoons orange marmalade

3 whole, raw turkey tenderloins, approximately the same size

1 egg beaten

1 cup corn flake crumbs OR seasoned dry bread crumbs

PROCEDURE

- In small saucepan combine apple, orange juice, cranberry sauce, and marmalade.
- Cook until apple is soft but holds its shape.
- Rinse tenderloins and pat dry.
- Slice them lengthwise, not all the way through, to form a pocket.
- Spoon some of the apple mixture into the pockets.
- Secure edges with toothpick or skewer.
- Dip tenderloins in beaten egg and then dredge in crumbs.
- Place in shallow baking dish so they do not touch.
- Bake at 350 degrees for 25 to 35 minutes.
- Heat remaining fruit mixture and serve over tenderloins.

NOTES

Serves 5 to 8.

POTATO-FROSTED TURKEY MEATLOAF

INGREDIENTS

Meat Loaf

1 pound ground turkey

1 egg

1/2 cup seasoned bread crumbs

1/4 cup water

1 tablespoon dried onions

1 tablespoon green peppers, chopped

1/8 teaspoon pepper

2 tablespoons ketchup

1 teaspoon prepared horseradish

1/2 teaspoon prepared mustard

Topping

4 servings of instant mashed potatoes

1/2 cup grated cheddar cheese

PROCEDURE

Meat Loaf

- Combine all ingredients.
- Place in lightly greased loaf pan.
- Bake at 350 degrees for 45 to 60 minutes or until meat is no longer pink in center. (Obviously it is difficult to see if the center is pink or not, so don't worry too much about this since turkey cooks quickly and should be cooked only until "just done.")
- Drain off any excess liquid.

Topping

- Frost loaf with mashed potatoes.
- Sprinkle with grated cheese.
- Return to oven and bake 5 minutes, or until cheese melts.

GRILLED TURKEY TENDERLOIN

INGREDIENTS

1 pound turkey tenderloins, 3/4 to 1 inch thick

1/4 cup soy sauce

1/4 cup vegetable oil

1/4 cup dry sherry

2 tablespoons pure lemon juice

2 tablespoons dehydrated onion

1/4 teaspoon ginger

Dash of black pepper

Dash of garlic salt

PROCEDURE

- Place turkey tenderloins in shallow pan.
- In small bowl, combine all other ingredients.
- Pour this marinade mixture over the turkey, turning to coat both sides.
- Cover and refrigerate several hours, turning occasionally.
- Grill tenderloins over hot coals for 6 to 8 minutes per side, depending on thickness.
- Turkey tenderloins are done when there is no pink in the center.
- Do not overcook.

NOTES

Serves 3 to 4. The source of most of these turkey recipes is the Wisconsin Department of Agriculture.

FOODS THROUGHOUT WISCONSIN
CHAPTER SEVEN

The following foods are common throughout Wisconsin and are not concentrated in any one particular region.

MILK

We have always known that milk is "nature's most perfect food," and those ads showing celebrities with their milk mustaches show we're in good company.

Wisconsin's claim to fame is that the 1.49 million dairy cows on its 27,346 dairy farms produce 14.7 percent of the entire U.S. milk supply. To move the entire annual production of 22.9 billion pounds of milk on one day would require a fleet of half a million trucks, each carrying 46,000 pounds of milk, or 92,000 glasses of milk. Not only does this conjure up a lot of milk mustaches but also one big milky traffic jam!

As America's Dairyland, Wisconsin has more milk cows than any other state—about 15.7 percent of the national total. On average, there are 54 cows per dairy farm and each cow produces about 1,800 gallons of milk per year.

Impressed with all these data? I am.

BUTTER

Butter dates back 3,500 years. Greeks and Romans applied it to their hair. Imagine taking a chariot ride on a hot day without a helmet! Somewhere, somehow, someone got the idea to "spread it on bread" and "not the head." Hurrah to that bit of civilized behavior modification.

Wisconsin never supplied legions of Romans, but its thirteen butter plants produce enough to rank Wisconsin second in the nation, supplying over 20 percent (about 280 million pounds) of the country's total butter supply. It takes 21.2 pounds of whole milk to make just one pound of butter.

Butter has three grades (check your carton): U.S. Grade AA, A, and B (which is certainly okay, but lacks some of the fine, fresh flavor of the other two).

Sweet cream butter (the usual table butter) is lightly salted and is especially good for making savory butters with herbs and wine. Unsalted butter (my favorite) is also known as sweet butter. Whipped butter spreads more easily than other butters because air has been incorporated in it, increasing the volume by approximately one third. It's better not to use whipped butter in baking because the recipe would have to be adjusted to compensate for the air factor.

If you want to spread butter on your hair as the Greeks and Romans did, well, okay, but I suggest you use margarine instead. Why waste good butter?

ICE CREAM

Although Wisconsin produces more than 19 million gallons of ice cream per year, it ranks only No. 22 in the nation. Still, if all of Wisconsin ice cream production were served up in ice cream cones, it would make a whopping 490 million cones—and many happy faces.

There should be no dietary guilt trip when eating ice cream since an average half-cup serving of vanilla (10 percent milkfat) has only 130 calories and super-premium vanilla (16 percent milkfat) has 175 calories. Compare that to a piece of chocolate cake with icing at 277 calories or a slice of apple pie at 404 calories. But forget the calories and enjoy some *postre* (Mexican fried ice cream): roll vanilla ice cream balls in a mixture of three parts sugar and one part cinnamon, then roll them in crushed frosted corn flakes. Freeze, and when ready to serve, place the balls in hot oil (375 degrees) for 4 seconds. Serve with Wisconsin honey or whipped cream. You'll love it!

EGGS

Wisconsin hens lay almost 900 million eggs per year (a mere twenty-sixth in the nation) with an economic value about $9 million.

A large egg is 95 percent fat free with only 70 calories. Egg sizes are classified according to minimum weight per dozen: jumbo eggs, 30 ounces per dozen; extra large, 27 ounces; medium, 21 ounces; and small, 18 ounces.

Grades are AA, A, and B, but all are equally nutritious. The difference in grades is based upon quality of the shell and interior (shape, firmness of yolk, proportion of thick to thin white).

Color of the shell has no effect on either nutrition or taste and results only from the breed of chicken.

To freeze eggs, blend the yolk and white, then transfer to freezer container.

Don't leave eggs out at room temperature for more than two hours.

The American Egg Board has coined the phrase "The Incredible, Edible Egg" and it certainly is all of that. Just think of all the ways eggs can be prepared, not to mention all the foods that would cease to exist if it weren't for eggs.

HONEY

Honey is known as the world's oldest luxury since bees have been making it for ten to twenty million years. Europeans brought honey bees to North America and Indians quickly dubbed them "white man's flies."

Honey is an extremely versatile ingredient, a natural sweetener, and fat free. Wisconsin produces almost six million pounds per year and is the tenth largest producer in the nation. Americans eat about 1.1 pounds of honey per capita per year.

A worker bee only makes about one twelfth of a teaspoon of honey in her lifetime, requiring stops at fifty to a hundred flowers per trip. For one pound of honey a bee racks up 40,000 miles and visits more than two million flowers. Honey flavor and color depend on what kind of flowers the bees visit. Generally, darker honey tastes stronger. Most of the three hundred types of honey are made from clover, which provides a very mild flavor.

Honey is the "nectar of the gods." It is 100 percent undiluted, 100 percent free of artificial chemicals or preservatives, and 100 percent absolutely scrumptious. When I say to my wife, "You'll always be my honey," she's never quite sure if I'm referring to her or my jar of honey.

VEGETABLES

Mothers all over the country are saying, "Eat your Wisconsin vegetables," because Wisconsin is so remarkably productive. It ranks first in beets (41 percent of the nation's total), third in both peas and carrots, and fourth in cucumbers. Furthermore, it ranks first in the processing of snap beans (31 percent of the nation's total) and third in sweet corn processing. And then there is the lima bean crop and the forty or fifty commercial shiitake mushrooms growers. No wonder Wisconsin devotes more acres to growing vegetables than any other state.

Peas have an interesting history: The ancient Norse believed that the pea was sent to man as punishment from the gods. Thor (the god of thunder) directed flying dragons to drop peas in the wells to rot and foul the water. But some of the peas fell in the fields and grew. Humans were so grateful that they dedicated the new vegetable to Thor and ate peas on his day—Thursday.

Then there was American humorist William Wallace Irwin, who said, "In the vegetable world, there is nothing so innocent, so confiding in its expression, as the small green face of the freshly shelled spring pea. Asparagus is pushy and bossy, lettuce is loud and blowzy, radishes are gay and playful, but the little green pea is so helpless and friendly that it makes really sensitive stomachs suffer to see how he is treated in the average home. Fling him into the water and let him boil—and that's that."

BERRIES

Wisconsin truck farms produce 5.5 million pounds of strawberries per year. That's enough to fill about 12 million eight-ounce jars with strawberry jam. Wisconsin ranks only tenth in strawberry production, but who cares? What's better than going to a local farm in early June to pick 'em completely red and fresh—one for the stomach and two for the basket until both are filled up.

Then there are raspberries, sometimes cultivated in small gardens but also found in the wild. The discovery of wild and wildly delicious raspberries makes the scratches from the bushes seem insignificant.

Another item high on the list of summer delights is the blueberry. Originally, native traders called them star berries because of the star-shaped calyx on the top of each one. In Wisconsin we likely to make blueberry muffins, pies, or pancakes. Folks in New England make dishes called "slump," "grunt," "buckle," or "cobbler." But they have no monopoly on the recipes for any one of them, so check your favorite cookbook if you feel like a little slump or grunt. I prefer my blueberries mixed in with my breakfast food, some half and half cream, and a sprinkling of sugar.

REFERENCES

ASSOCIATIONS, ORGANIZATIONS, AND BUSINESSES

The fine folks in the organizations below are experts in their respective food areas, and I relied on their vast knowledge in preparing this book. My readers deserve to know the companies that manufacture fine Wisconsin foods and the organizations that represent and promote them.

Ambrosia Chocolate Co., Milwaukee, Wisconsin

American Dairy Association, Brownsdale, Minnesota

Arm and Hammer, Division of Church and Swight Co., Princeton, New Jersey

Bublitz's Family Restaurant, Saukville, Wisconsin

Burlington Chamber of Commerce, Burlington, Wisconsin

Captain Ezra Nye House, Sandwich, Massachusetts

Chieftain Wild Rice Co., Spooner, Wisconsin

Country Ovens, Forestville, Wisconsin

Dairy Council of Wisconsin, Brookfield, Wisconsin

Fremont Co., Fremont, Ohio

Gourmet Center, Greendale, Wisconsin

Hsu's Ginseng Enterprises, Wausau, Wisconsin

Jones Sausage Co., Ft. Atkinson, Wisconsin

Klement's, Milwaukee, Wisconsin

Maple Leaf Farms, Milford, Indiana

Miller Brewing Co., Milwaukee, Wisconsin

National Pork Board, Des Moines, Iowa

National Pork Producers Council, Des Moines, Iowa

Nestlé, Burlington, Wisconsin

Pabst Brewing Co., Milwaukee, Wisconsin

Provimi Veal, Waukesha, Wisconsin

Reynolds Sugar Bush, Inc., Aniwa, Wisconsin

Sheboygan Sausage Co., Sheboygan, Wisconsin

United States Department of Agriculture, Washington, D.C.

University of Wisconsin Extension, Madison, Wisconsin

Usinger's, Milwaukee, Wisconsin

Wisconsin Apple Growers Association, Oregon, Wisconsin

Wisconsin Association of Meat Processors, Lodi, Wisconsin

Wisconsin Bakers Association, Milwaukee, Wisconsin

Wisconsin Beef Council, Madison, Wisconsin

Wisconsin Berry Growers Association, Lodi, Wisconsin

Wisconsin Cattlemen's Association, Madison, Wisconsin

Wisconsin Cheese & Specialty Food Merchants Association, Madison, Wisconsin

Wisconsin Cheese Makers Association, Madison, Wisconsin

Wisconsin Cranberry Festival, Warrens, Wisconsin

Wisconsin Dairy Producers Association, Middleton, Wisconsin

Wisconsin Department of Agriculture, Trade and Consumer Protection, Marketing Division, Madison, Wisconsin

Wisconsin Department of Natural Resources, Fish Advisory, Madison, Wisconsin

Wisconsin Egg Producers Association, Lake Mills, Wisconsin

Wisconsin Fresh Market Vegetable Growers Association, Winneconne, Wisconsin

Wisconsin Ginseng Growers Association, Marathon, Wisconsin

Wisconsin Honey Producers Association, Ogdensburg, Wisconsin

Wisconsin Maple Syrup Producers Association, Holcombe, Wisconsin

Wisconsin Milk Marketing Board, Madison, Wisconsin

Wisconsin Pork Producers, Lancaster, Wisconsin

Wisconsin Potato and Vegetable Growers Association, Antigo, Wisconsin

Wisconsin Potato Growers Auxiliary, Inc., Antigo, Wisconsin

Wisconsin Potato Industry Board, Antigo, Wisconsin

Wisconsin Red Cherry Growers Association, Baileys Harbor, Wisconsin

Wisconsin State Cranberry Growers Association, Wisconsin Rapids, Wisconsin

Wisconsin Swiss and Limburger Cheese, Monroe, Wisconsin

Wisconsin Turkey Federation, Chilton, Wisconsin

Wisconsin Veal Growers Association, Dorchester, Wisconsin

BOOKS, ARTICLES, AND BOOKLETS

Academics call it research. All writers, lecturers, and other people who wish to be knowledgeable about a subject must draw upon the wisdom, experience, and research of others. These are some of the sources I have consulted over the years to extend my knowledge of food and cooking.

Adams, Charlotte. *Cooking with Style*. Garden City, N.Y.: Doubleday, 1967.

The All-American Potato Cookbook. Elmsford, N.Y.: Benjamin Co., 1982.

Apps, Jerry. *Cheese: The Making of a Wisconsin Tradition*. Amherst, Wis.: Amherst Press, 1998.

Bratfold, Gretchen. *Wisconsin*. Minneapolis: Lerner Publications, 1991.

Brown, Bob. *The Complete Book of Cheese*. New York: Gramercy Publishing, 1959.

Cook's and Diner's Dictionary. New York: Funk and Wagnalls, 1968.

Degouy, Louis P. *The Derrydale Fish Cook Book*. New York: Derrydale Press, 1937.

Funk, Wilford. *Word Origins*. Avenel, N.J.: Wings Books, 1950.

Hachten, Harva. *The Flavor of Wisconsin*. Madison: State Historical Society of Wisconsin, 1986.

Game and Fish, Their Preparation and Special Cooking. St. Paul, Minn.: Brown and Bigelow, 1960.

Gard, Robert, and L.G. Sorden. *The Romance of Wisconsin Placenames*. Minocqua, Wis.: Heartland Press, 1988.

Give Us This Day Our Daily Bread. Washington Island, Wis.: Trinity Lutheran Women of the Church, 1959.

Guide to Wisconsin Counties (1848-1998). Sesquicentennial Issue, Limited Edition. Washington, D.C.:
    U.S. Postal Service, 1998.

Herbst, Sharon Tyler. *Food Lover's Companion*. New York: Barron's, 1990.

Hintz, Martin and Dan. *Wisconsin: Off the Beaten Path*. 2d ed. Old Saybrook, Conn.: Globe, Pequot Press, 1992.

Holmes, Fred L. *Old World Wisconsin*. Minocqua, Wis.: Heartland Press, 1944.

Kander, Mrs. Simon, and Schoenfeld, Mrs. Henry, compilers. *The "Settlement" Cookbook: The Way to a Man's Heart*,
    1903, reprint. New York: New American Library, 1985.

Kimball, Yeffe, and Jean Anderson. *The Art of American Indian Cooking*. New York: Simon and Schuster, 1986.

Krohn, Norman Odya. *Menu Mystique: The Diner's Guide to Fine Food and Drink*. Middle Village, N.Y.:
    Jonathan David Publishers, 1983.

Let's Travel: Pathways Through Wisconsin. St. Paul, Minn.: Clark and Miles, 1995.

"Making It Big in Wisconsin," *Milwaukee Journal*, September 5, 1993.

INDEX

A

Adults Only Chocolate Sauce, 41
Amaretto Apples with Meringue, 58
Apple(s)
    and Butternut Squash Soup, 50
    and Cabbage, German-Style, 55
    Bread, 53
    Butter, 54
    Cake, Maple Syrup, 99
    Cheese Crisp, Nutty, 57
    Crunch, 56
    Pie, Cranberry, 129
    Pie, Old-Fashioned, 67
    Quiche, Cheese, 153
    Salad, Heavenly, 51
    Salad, Potato, 135
    -Stuffed Turkey Tenderloin, 191
    with Meringue, Amaretto, 58
Applesauce Muffins, Oat Bran, 52

B

Baked Muskie, 168
Beef
    Craisin-Glazed, 128
    Ginseng and, 119
    Mincemeat Pie, 69
    Sauerkraut Cranberry Meatballs, 22
    Stew, Cranberry, 126
    Wild Rice Hamburger Casserole, 182
Beer
    Batter, 6
    Batter, Quick, 7
    Biscuits, Extra-Light, 5
    Bloody Mary, 14
    Cheese Dip, 12
    Cheese Fondue, 155
    Cheese Soup, 4
    Cheese Spread, 13
    Chicken in, 9
    Cookies, 11
    Ham Baked with, 8
    Shrimp in, 10
Beverages
    Beer Bloody Mary, 14
    Dieter's Maple Power Shake, 95
    Mulled Cherry Grog, 111
Biscuits, Extra-Light Beer, 5
Bologna
    Casserole, Full of, 81
    Hors d'Oeuvres, Pickled, 80
Bourbon Pecan Pie, 71
Bratwurst Hors d'Oeuvres, 79
Bread
    Apple, 53
    Cheese, 148
    Cranberry Nut, 124
    Easy Maple Nut, 96
    Sticks, Mashed Potato, 134
Brewed Sauerkraut, 18
Brunswick Stew, Original, 175
Butter
    Apple, 54
    Maple Whipped, 97
Butter-Simmered Onions, 78

C

Cabbage, German-Style Apples and, 55
Cake
    Chocolate Sauerkraut, 23
    Cranberry, with Caramel Sauce, 130
    Loosey-Moussey Chocolate, 33
    Maple Syrup Apple, 99
Candy
    Chocolate Butter Crunch, 39
    Chocolate Truffles, 40
    Maple Copycat (Kit-Kat) Bars, 98
    Maple Fudge, 102
    Potato, 143
    Spudnut Kisses, 142
Casserole
    Full of Bologna, 81
    Reuben Sausage, 84
    Sauerkraut Potato, 19
    Scalloped Potatoes in Wine, 139
    Wild Rice Chicken, 184
    Wild Rice Hamburger, 182

Wisconsin Farmhouse Cheese Supper, 151

Cheese(s)

and Deviled Ham Hors d'Oeuvres, 146

Apple Quiche, 153

Blue Cheese Cucumber Salad, Wisconsin, 149

Bread, 148

Chocolate Cream Cheese Pie, 37

Crisp, Nutty Apple, 57

Cucumber Salad, Wisconsin Blue, 149

Dip, Beer, 12

Fondue, Beer, 155

Golden Oven-Roasted Potatoes and, 137

Hors d'Oeuvres, Cheese-Covered Grape, 145

Macaroni-Cheese-Ham Salad, 150

Maple Syrup Dip/Topping, 100

Mashed Potatoes, Three-Cheese, 140

Pretzels, Soft, 154

Soufflé, Never-Fail, 152

Soup

Beer, 4

Potato-Broccoli-, 133

Spread, 147

Spread, Beer, 13

Supper, Wisconsin Farm House, 151

Cheesecake

Creamy Baked, 156

Fudge Truffle, 35

Cherry(ies)

Cobbler, Door County, 104

Creme Pie, Chocolate, 107

Crunch, 108

Dream Bars, 109

Grog, Mulled, 111

Jubilee, 112

Oat Bran Muffins, Dried, 110

Torte, 105

Torte, No-Bake, 106

Chicken

Casserole, Wild Rice, 184

in Beer, 9

Chocolate

Butter Crunch Candy, 39

Cake, Loosey-Moussey, 33

Cherry Creme Pie, 107

Cream Cheese Pie, 37

Milk Chocolate Terrine, 36

Sauce, Adults Only, 41

Sauerkraut Cake, 23

Truffles, 40

Chocolate Chip

Cookies, Wisconsin State Fair Giant, 38

Marshmallow Torte, 34

Cobbler, Door County Cherry, 104

Coleslaw, Cranberry, 122

Cookies

Beer, 11

Potato Chip, 141

Wisconsin State Fair Giant Chocolate Chip, 38

Cornish Pasties, 63

Craisin-Glazed Steak, 128

Cranberry(ies)

Apple Pie, 129

Beef Stew, 126

Cake with Caramel Sauce, 130

Coleslaw, 122

Craisin-Glazed Steak, 128

Jubilee, 131

Meatballs, Sauerkraut, 22

Nut Bread, 124

Pork Chops, 127

Salad or Dessert, Frozen, 123

Turkey Tacos, 125

Cream Puff(s)

Miniature Crabmeat-Filled, 30

Swans, 31

Wisconsin State Fair, 29

Creamy Baked Cheesecake, 156

Creamy Reuben Soup, 16

Crock Pot Duck with Grand Marnier Orange Sauce, 45

Cucumber Salad, Wisconsin Blue Cheese, 149

D

Dieter's Maple Power Shake, 95

Door County Cherry Cobbler, 104

Dried Cherry Oat Bran Muffins, 110

Duck

Enchiladas, 44
　with Grand Marnier Orange Sauce, Crock Pot, 45
　with Sauerkraut, 43
Dumplings
　Potato, 61
　Swiss Spaetzle, 60
　Venison with Bread Dumplings, 174

E

Easy Maple Nut Bread, 96
Easy Shoo-Fly Pie, 70
Extra-Light Beer Biscuits, 5

F

Fajitas, Turkey, 190
Fish/Seafood
　Crabmeat-Filled Cheese Puffs, Miniature, 30
　Fish Boil, Indoor, 114
　Fish Fry, Friday Night, 166
　Lake Trout, Poached, 170
　Muskie, Baked, 168
　Pan-Fried, 167
　Shrimp in Beer, 10
　Walleye, Grilled Amaretto-Basted, 169
Friday Night Fish Fry, 166
Frozen Cranberry Salad or Dessert, 123
Fudge, Maple, 102
Fudge Truffle Cheesecake, 35
Full of Bologna Casserole, 81

G

German Potato Salad, 136
German-Style Apples and Cabbage, 55
Ginseng
　and Beef, 119
　Salad, Tossed, 120
　Sex Muffins, 118
Golden Oven-Roasted Potatoes and Cheese, 137
Granola, Maple, 94
Grilled Amaretto-Basted Walleye, 169
Grilled Turkey Tenderloin, 193

H

Ham
　Baked with Beer, 8
　Deviled Ham Hors d'Oeuvres, Cheese and, 146
　Salad, Macaroni-Cheese-, 150
　Salad, Wild Rice, 181
Heavenly Apple Salad, 51
Hodag Pie, 164
Hors d'Oeuvres/Dips/Spreads
　Apple Butter, 54
　Beer Cheese Dip, 12
　Beer Cheese Spread, 13
　Bratwurst Hors d'Oeuvres, 79
　Cheese and Deviled Ham Hors d'Oeuvres, 146
　Cheese-Covered Grape Hors d'Oeuvres, 145
　Cheese Spread, 147
　Crabmeat-Filled Cream Puffs, Miniature, 30
　Hot Venison Spread, 173
　Maple Syrup Dip/Topping, 100
　Maple Whipped Butter, 97
　Pickled Bologna Hors d'Oeuvres, 80
　Sauerkraut Dip/Sauce, 24
Horseradish Sauce # l, 186
Horseradish Sauce # 2, 187
Hot Dogs
　Oven-Barbecued, 83
　with Original Coney Island Sauce, 82
Hot Venison Spread, 173

I

Indoor Fish Boil, 114

J

Jerky, Venison, 172
Johnny Cake, 162

K

Kielbasa Pasta Salad, 85
Kisses, Spudnut, 142
Kringle
　No-Yeast, 27
　Quick and Easy Danish, 26

L

Lake Trout, Poached, 170
Lefse, 73
Loosey-Moussey Chocolate Cake, 33

M

Macaroni-Cheese-Ham Salad, 150
Maple
    Copycat (Kit-Kat) Bars, 98
    Fudge, 102
    -Glazed Breakfast Sausage, 87
    Granola, 94
    Nut Bread, Easy, 96
    Pecan Pie, 101
    Power Shake, Dieter's, 95
    Whipped Butter, 97
Maple Syrup
    Apple Cake, 99
    Dip/Topping, 100
Mashed Potato(es)
    Balls, 138
    Bread Sticks, 134
    Three-Cheese, 140
Milk Chocolate Terrine, 36
Mincemeat Pie, 69
Miniature Crabmeat-Filled Cream Puffs, 30
Muerbe Teig Pie Crust, 66
Muffins
    Dried Cherry Oat Bran, 110
    Oat Bran Applesauce, 52
    Sex, 118
Mulled Cherry Grog, 111
Muskie, Baked, 168

N

Never-Fail Cheese Soufflé, 152
No-Bake Cherry Torte, 106
No-Yeast Kringle, 27
Nutty Apple Cheese Crisp, 57

O

Oat Bran Applesauce Muffins, 52
Old-Fashioned Apple Pie, 67

Onions, Butter-Simmered, 78
Original Brunswick Stew, 175
Oven-Barbecued Hot Dogs, 83

P

Pan-Fried Fish, 167
Pasta
    Salad, Kielbasa, 85
Pasties
    Cornish, 63
    Welsh, 64
Pheasant, 176
Pickled Bologna Hors d'Oeuvres, 80
Pie(s)
    Apple, Old-Fashioned, 67
    Bourbon Pecan, 71
    Chocolate Cherry Creme, 107
    Chocolate Cream Cheese, 37
    Cranberry Apple, 129
    Crust, Muerbe Teig, 66
    Easy Shoo-Fly, 70
    Hodag, 164
    Maple Pecan, 101
    Mincemeat, 69
    Shoepac, 160
    Sour Cream Prune, 68
Poached Lake Trout, 170
Pork Chops
    Cranberry, 127
    Sauerkraut, 21
Pork, Stir-Fry Wild Rice, Snow Peas, and, 183
Potato(es)
    and Cheese, Golden Oven-Roasted, 137
    Apple Salad, 135
    -Broccoli-Cheese Soup, 133
    Candy, 143
    Casserole, Sauerkraut, 19
    Dumplings, 61
    -Frosted Turkey Meat Loaf, 192
    in Wine, Scalloped, 139
    Lefse, 73
    Mashed Potato Balls, 138
    Mashed Potato Bread Sticks, 134

Salad, German, 136
Spudnut Kisses, 142
Three-Cheese Mashed, 140
Potato Chip Cookies, 141
Pretzels, Soft Cheese, 154
Prune Pie, Sour Cream, 68

Q

Quick and Easy Danish Kringle, 26
Quick Beer Batter, 7

R

Reuben Sausage Casserole, 84

S

Salad(s)
Cranberry Coleslaw, 122
Cranberry Salad or Dessert, Frozen, 123
German Potato, 136
Heavenly Apple, 51
Kielbasa Pasta, 85
Macaroni-Cheese-Ham, 150
Potato Apple, 135
Sauerkraut, 17
Sausage Tostado, 86
Tossed Ginseng, 120
Wild Rice Ham, 181
Wisconsin Blue Cheese Cucumber, 149
Sauce(s)
Caramel Sauce, Cranberry Cake with, 130
Cherries Jubilee, 112
Chocolate Sauce, Adults Only, 41
Cranberries Jubilee, 131
Grand Marnier Orange Sauce, Crock Pot Duck with, 45
Horseradish Sauce # l, 186
Horseradish Sauce # 2, 187
Maple Syrup Dip/Topping, 100
Original Coney Island Sauce, Hot Dogs with, 82
Sauerkraut Dip/Sauce, 24
Sauerkraut
Brewed, 18
Cake, Chocolate, 23
Cranberry Meatballs, 22

Creamy Reuben Soup, 16
Dip/Sauce, 24
Duck with, 43
in Wine, 20
Pork Chops, 21
Potato Casserole, 19
Salad, 17
Sausage
Bratwurst Hors d'Oeuvres, 79
Full of Bologna Casserole, 81
Hot Dogs
Oven-Barbecued, 83
with Original Coney Island Sauce, 82
Kielbasa Pasta Salad, 85
Maple-Glazed Breakfast, 87
Pickled Bologna Hors d'Oeuvres, 80
Reuben Sausage Casserole, 84
Tostado Salad, 86
Scalloped Potatoes in Wine, 139
Scaloppini, Veal, 89
Sex Muffins, 118
Shake, Dieter's Maple Power, 95
Shoepac Pie, 160
Shrimp in Beer, 10
Snow Peas and Pork, Stir Fry Wild Rice, 183
Soft Cheese Pretzels, 154
Soufflé, Never-Fail Cheese, 152
Soup
Apple and Butternut Squash, 50
Beer Cheese, 4
Creamy Reuben, 16
Potato-Broccoli-Cheese, 133
Wild Rice, 180
Sour Cream Prune Pie, 68
Spaetzle, Swiss, 60
Spudnut Kisses, 142
Squash Soup, Apple and Butternut, 50
Steak, Craisin-Glazed, 128
Stew
Cranberry Beef, 126
Original Brunswick, 175
Veal, 92
Stir-Fry Wild Rice, Snow Peas, and Pork, 183

Swans, Cream Puff, 31
Swiss Spaetzle, 60

T

Tacos, Cranberry Turkey, 125
Terrine, Milk Chocolate, 36
Three-Cheese Mashed Potatoes, 140
Torte
    Cherry, 105
    Cherry, No-Bake, 106
    Chocolate Chip Marshmallow, 34
Tossed Ginseng Salad, 120
Truffles, Chocolate, 40
Turkey
    Fajitas, 190
    Joes, 189
    Meat Loaf, Potato-Frosted, 192
    Tacos, Cranberry, 125
    Tenderloin
        Apple-Stuffed, 191
        Grilled, 193

V

Veal
    Loaf, 91
    Scaloppini, 89
    Stew, 92
    Wiener Schnitzel, 90
Venison
    Jerky, 172
    Spread, Hot, 173
    with Bread Dumplings, 174

W

Walleye, Grilled Amaretto-Basted, 169
Welsh Pasties, 64
Wiener Schnitzel, 90
Wild Rice
    Chicken Casserole, 184
    Hamburger Casserole, 182
    Ham Salad, 181
    Snow Peas and Pork, Stir-Fry, 183
    Soup, 180

Wisconsin Blue Cheese Cucumber Salad, 149
Wisconsin Farm House Cheese Supper, 151
Wisconsin State Fair Cream Puffs, 29
Wisconsin State Fair Giant Chocolate Chip Cookies, 38